More Praise for *Smart or Lucky?*

"In her fascinating book *Smart or Lucky?*, Judith Hurwitz recounts many of the companies and characters whose innovations and luck (or lack thereof) have made the information technology industry what it is today. As someone who knew many of the actors and even played a small part in the drama, I found this a fascinating and illuminating read. I recommend it highly to budding entrepreneurs and others who want to understand the industry and how it works, and who want to learn from its past so they can repeat its successes but avoid its failures."
—John Swainson, former CEO, CA Inc.

"This book should be required reading for all technology start-ups and their investors. Judith Hurwitz has captured some of the history and a great deal of the spirit of our industry's evolution. She most poignantly describes how some of the most successful tech companies suddenly found themselves in a world of hurt. *Smart or Lucky?* is a guidepost to help current and future entrepreneurs avoid the sins of the past."
—Alan Nugent, former CTO, Novell and CA, Inc.

"As someone who has watched thousands of technology firms come and go, Judith Hurwitz has rare insight into the dynamics that shape technology markets. Whether you're a newcomer to the field or a grizzled veteran, read this book to understand how to survive in a cutthroat business that is only becoming more unforgiving."
—Paul Gillin, author, *The New Influencers and Secrets of Social Media Marketing*

"I've worked with some of the smartest and luckiest people in High Tech, and I am now certain that luck is intentionally created via pattern recognition, partnerships, and paying attention. Want to create a revolution, empire, or industry standard? Read this book. It provides the formula for smarts + luck."
—Christine Comaford, CEO, coach and author, *Rules for Renegades*

SMART OR LUCKY?

How Technology Leaders Turn Chance into Success

JUDITH HURWITZ

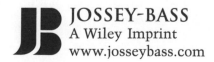

JOSSEY-BASS
A Wiley Imprint
www.josseybass.com

Library of Congress Cataloging-in-Publication Data

Hurwitz, Judith.
  Smart or lucky? : how technology leaders turn chance into success / Judith Hurwitz. — 1st ed.
    p. cm.
  Includes index.
    ISBN 978-0-470-89142-1 (hardback), 978-1-118-03378-4 (ebk), 978-1-118-03379-1 (ebk), 978-1-118-03381-4 (ebk)
  1. Entrepreneurship. 2. Businesspeople. 3. High technology industries.
  4. Technological innovations. 5. Success in business. 6. Sustainable development. I. Title.
  HB615.H87 2011
  658.4'01—dc22

                                                                    2010053639

Printed in the United States of America

FIRST EDITION

HB Printing 10 9 8 7 6 5 4 3 2 1

I dedicate this book to my family:
my husband Warren,
my parents Elaine and David,
my children Sara and David.

CONTENTS

INTRODUCTION: SMART OR LUCKY?

For the past three decades, I have been lucky enough to work in the most exciting industry in the world. The amount of innovation in technology over the past several decades is unparalleled in history. During this time, we have gone from a single computer system that consumed city blocks to a world of iPads and smartphones that enable people to communicate across continents in an instant. The pace of innovation in other industries pales in comparison with the rapidity of growth in high tech. If, for example, the automobile industry had changed as fast as the computer industry has changed, your family car would now cost but a few hundred dollars, it would be pollution free, and it would last a lifetime.

But the growth of the computer industry is not a simple story. It is a tale of brilliant individuals and teams who came up with ideas that fundamentally changed the world of business. Some of these teams were so far ahead of the needs of the market that they faded into history without realizing their dreams, because the market just wasn't ready for them. Therefore, this book is less about pure innovation and more about luck, good fortune, and the smarts necessary to sustain that good fortune.

I have watched thousands of companies come and go, from the earliest firms that almost no one remembers—like Univac, Burroughs, Commodore, Altair, Prime Computer, Data General, and Wang Laboratories—to the newer companies like AltaVista, Netscape, Excite, and Lycos. Although none of these companies exists today, they all combined initial luck with lots of innovation. They just couldn't sustain their success over more than a few decades. In their day, these were hugely powerful and profitable companies, but none of them managed to last longer than thirty years. Different companies, but common themes: each was lucky enough to be in the right place at the right time, each became overly arrogant or consumed by internal politics, and each failed to adapt to changing circumstances.

This book sets forth what I have learned over the past thirty years about sustaining success in business. It describes both stunningly successful high-tech companies like Google and disappointing failures like Wang. What did the successful companies have in common that the failures lacked? Companies that are successful focus on *innovation*, *pragmatism*, and *radical change*.

Innovation matters. Innovation is key to staying ahead of the competition. Successful companies are highly innovative and challenge market incumbents by changing customer expectations. But innovation isn't enough. Pragmatism keeps a company grounded in solving customer needs in the current market. Innovation is valuable only when and if it solves customer problems—either today or sometime in the future. If a company develops an innovative technology for the sake of demonstrating cleverness, before long it becomes just an interesting footnote in a fast-changing story, not a game changer. And successful companies change. These companies create a long-term roadmap that anticipates change. Companies that fail to change because they grow too attached to their existing products are doomed to fail. Companies that withstand the pressures of competition and changing technologies are those that innovate, solve customer problems, and are prepared to change as markets evolve.

I had the good fortune to start my career as a computer journalist during a fascinating transitional period in the computer industry. In 1978, the industry was on the cusp of huge change, from mainframe computing to minicomputers and personal computers. Software was not viewed as a revenue source or an independent industry; it was created only to help sell extremely profitable hardware. Computers lacked color and graphics. No one in their wildest dreams imagined the world that we now take for granted—with seemingly omniscient search engines and cloud computing, with everything from personal photographs to accounting software to word processing available with a simple Internet connection. With the power of cloud computing, scientists can now collaborate on research with colleagues across the globe. But that wasn't always the case. Video conferencing was the stuff of science fiction. I watched new technology come out of nowhere, springing from the imagination and creativity of super smart people who not only had great ideas but whose timing was perfect. These people were able to recognize needs, capitalize on them, and surpass the competition. I watched the CEOs of companies that were about to be supplanted smirk at the seeming insignificance of a brash upstart that had the audacity to challenge their supremacy. I have watched companies with incredibly creative and innovative ideas fail—and other companies with similar ideas succeed a decade later.

The leaders of some upstart companies were able to turn markets upside down because they leveraged emerging technology that had been percolating in obscurity for decades and offered solutions to problems that had seemed insurmountable. Often these companies weren't the only ones to come up with these ideas, but they either executed them more deftly than their competitors or were just in the right place at the right time. The lucky companies grew large, powerful, and successful, but as their success continued, they often lost sight of how they had achieved their success in the first place. Their leaders began to think that they were invincible. Their companies got bogged down in internal political battles for power. They decided they did not need to listen to customers or change their strategies in any way. Sometimes they listened too closely to customers, corrected minor problems, and lost sight of the needs of those same customers. As they grew powerful and complacent, new companies—without a legacy of products and customers to worry about and with some new ideas and better execution—took over market leadership.

Of course, this doesn't always happen. Some companies get a wakeup call and manage to avoid the pitfalls of complacency and bureaucratization. That wakeup call can be a bad financial result or a promising product that fails. Companies that learn how to overcome setbacks and adapt to new environments seem more able to combine an effective growth strategy with their good luck.

So how can we explain the varying fortunes of companies in a complicated market like technology? Why does one technology company thrive while another with equally smart people slips into obscurity? There is no simple answer. There are many different factors that determine success or failure in business, but my experience has taught me that the companies who succeed are the ones that combine luck with smart execution.

Because I'm talking so much about luck and smarts, it's important to define what I mean when using these terms. "Luck" means that your technology comes to market at just the right time, when customers are ready to adopt it. "Smart" means that you are able to appreciate the opportunity you have in the marketplace, you figure out how to capitalize on that opportunity, and you execute well through many stages of maturation. You learn to listen for customers' unsolved problems, to pay attention to the market dynamics, and to plan for the long term. You also learn when to listen to your customers and when *not* to listen. Conversely, you recognize that sometimes your critics might be right. The difference between those companies that have longevity in the market and those that don't is that the successful ones leave their egos at the door and listen to their detractors.

There are plenty of smart people in the world. But being smart isn't enough. After almost thirty years of working with entrepreneurs, I can tell you that innovation alone rarely guarantees success. On the contrary, success in the business of technology requires a combination of intuition, persistence, intelligence, and teamwork, as well as luck. Luck often plays a bigger role in the early success of a company than anyone likes to believe. For example, many early Internet search companies hired brilliant computer scientists who created incredible technology. Yet companies like Inktomi and AltaVista went out of business or were sold for a fraction of their earlier value. Enterprise computing companies such as Sun Microsystems, with all of their advanced technology, could not sustain their market position and in the end either were acquired or went out of business. Other companies, like Apple, Inc., and Microsoft, started out as niche desktop computer players and were then able to transform themselves into innovative juggernauts. Lucky companies bring excellent products to market at exactly the time when there is a demand for those products. Smart companies recognize that that initial lucky phase is just the opening stage of a long journey. They recognize the element of luck in their success and understand that they must harness their luck, build on that spark, and move quickly to take advantage of their window of opportunity.

Furthermore, all types of luck are not the same. For example, if you go to a casino and play the roulette wheel, you might get lucky and hit a winning number. There is no advance planning involved. This is not the type of luck I am talking about. Taking advantage of luck in the high-tech world includes the following elements, which I discuss in greater detail throughout the book:

- You understand your customers and know what will solve their problems right now.

- You have a roadmap to follow if you gain market traction.

- You don't overengineer your products. Products need to be good enough to solve customers' problems and stay ahead of the competition but not so complex that customers are intimidated.

- You don't worry about immediate success. You focus on how you will succeed after competitors challenge your market position.

- You worry continuously about being in the right place at the right time.

- You worry about innovation only if it makes your customers successful.

- You care more about commercial success than about simply being famous.

- You are patient. You are willing to get some quick hits to put your company on the map, but you also have a long-term strategy. You can always answer the question: what's next?

- You aren't afraid of change. You aren't afraid to kill a once-successful product that is holding you back from investing in the future.

- You are keenly aware of your luck. You don't believe your own marketing hype. You are realistic and honest about why you have been successful and what challenges lie ahead.

Because of the fast pace of the technology market, it is easy to assume that all new ideas come from the imaginations of brilliant young entrepreneurs. However, the best way to ensure success is to learn the lessons of history. In this book, I examine key questions about success in the world of high tech. Why have companies like IBM, HP, Apple, and Microsoft been able to thrive over the long haul? What are emerging leaders such as Google, Amazon.com, salesforce.com, and hundreds of others teaching us about the path to success? How has the ascent of cloud computing accelerated the trajectory of companies that enter the market and either succeed or fail within years rather than decades?

Many factors determine business success. This book contains the lessons I have learned from others' successes and failures. The common denominator is this: Success requires a combination of luck and smarts. When luck and smarts come together, magic can happen.

In the ten chapters that follow, we'll explore the following themes:

1. Don't take your luck for granted. Know when you have been lucky enough to be in the right place at the right time. Too often, companies that achieve success become arrogant and complacent. It is wonderful to have great fortune, but you also need to be smart enough to leverage that luck and sustain your competitive advantage.

2. Make it easy for customers to get started. The most innovative technology can and probably will be intimidating. If a technology is really important, customers will put up with a lot of pain because they feel they must use the technology to gain an advantage over competitors. However, customers must be able to recognize the value of this technology before they will invest both time and money. Once you convince customers that there is huge business value in your products, customers will take the time to learn how to use them effectively and integrate them into their businesses. Once this happens, customers rarely walk away. They tend to remain customers for a long time.

3. Fail often in order to succeed sooner. Some of the most successful companies are those that have had near death experiences. Likewise, some of the most successful entrepreneurs are those who have a few failures under their belt. The trick is to learn from your failures and become smarter.

4. Strategize to fool complacent competitors. In complex markets with strong and powerful competitors, it is important to gain customer and market traction—before challenging your competitors. Create a persona for your company that threatens no one—at least until you are ready to attack. With a sneaky strategy, you can position yourself for growth and even sustainability before your competitors can put you out of business.

5. Make customers a part of your success. You have to make the most influential individuals who work for your customers successful. An individual's success may result in a promotion, better skills, a new job, or internal recognition. These individuals become an extension of your sales force and can propel you forward to great heights. On the other hand, if you cause customers to fail, they will let everyone know; if that happens too often, you become the proverbial toast.

6. Have a plan for how you can apply your technology to immediately address customer pain. Some sophisticated technologists believe that great technology will be appreciated just because it is great. However, some companies, despite having lots of money and brilliant inventions, never get off the ground because they don't have a plan for how and to what effect the technology can actually be used. What they lack is the answer to the question: "What does your technology allow me to do that I couldn't do before?" The response must not be: "How can you not appreciate the innovative technology we have developed?"

7. Create actual business solutions. Simply creating a plan to sell technology isn't enough. You need to package that technology so that it addresses the problems that customers are solving within their specific industry or discipline. Too often companies solve only one aspect of a difficult technology problem. The technology industry is littered with supposed innovations that turned out to be merely passing fads or steppingstones to something bigger. To be successful, you have to be smart enough to recognize when you have a true solution to a business problem.

8. Don't be fooled into thinking there is such a thing as an overnight success. Successful technology companies are built on the shoulders of pioneers with great ideas that were ahead of their time. If you are lucky enough to be able to take a great idea and bring it to market at the right time, you can win. But being lucky isn't enough. Once you get your lucky break, ongoing success requires hard work, persistence, execution, and imagination. Without these things, your success will be short-lived.

9. Always stay a few steps ahead of your customers. Even if customers think your products are the best they've ever

seen, you cannot rest on your laurels. The technology graveyard is filled with companies that were "hot" for a short while and then faded away as quickly as they emerged. Smart companies that survive keep innovating and anticipate shifts in market demand even before they happen.

10. Don't be afraid to destroy your existing cash cow products in order to create a sustainable future. Too many companies keep moving forward with outdated products for fear of losing short-term revenue. If you do this, your competition will easily get the better of you with new and better products. Smart companies keep reinventing their products and themselves.

Companies that get a lucky break can change an industry. For every company like a Google, an Apple, Inc., or an IBM that made it big, there have been hundreds, maybe even thousands of companies and computer engineers with similarly great ideas who never succeeded. The difference is a combination of persistence, execution, imagination, and a lot of luck.

A common thread runs through the stories of companies that are unable to sustain their success for very long. When a company begins to rule its domain, it doesn't imagine that its luck can possibly run out. In fact, it may never see its success as having anything to do with luck. The founders and top executives are and always have been the smartest guys in the room, and they know it. Some of them had success with an earlier venture, and they assume that anything they touch will surely turn to gold.

I have seen many companies that did not know how to create sustainability after their initial success. They lacked the insight and strategy to persist because they lost sight of what was important. These companies tend to be dominated by management teams with some common characteristics:

- *They lack perspective.* The top executives have some success with a product and assume that their success is solely due to their brilliance.

- *They believe their own hype.* The company assembles a great marketing team that creates a story about the company and its success. They then begin to believe their own hype without executing well on the long-term strategy.

- *They dismiss potential competitors.* When a new startup comes into their market, the market incumbent underestimates and dismisses its potential.

- *They act without proper planning.* When faced with emerging threats, they panic and react quickly and without a plan. They may add too many new features and functions to their products based on customer input, or they may quickly attempt to copy what they see their competitors selling without really considering if this is the right path for the company to take.

- *They are too focused on the present.* These companies spend so much time worrying about existing competitors and the current market that they miss the next big thing.

- *They get complacent.* They look only at the number of customers they have now; they listen only to those who are eager to flatter them.

Early success, especially in technology markets, can be seductive. It is easy to get caught up in the excitement and forget about planning for the future. In fact, early luck can sometimes blind the most seasoned business leader into complacency.

In these pages, I examine companies that got lucky by being in the right place at the right time but were never able to translate that luck into long-term success. I also look at companies that were lucky and then used that luck to make the right moves to sustain growth over time. The differences between the two can be subtle. It is human nature to get too close to your own products and your own marketing strategies and lose sight of the future. In complicated technology markets, you not only need a well-designed technology platform based on the experience of the smartest minds in the business, but you also have to combine this technology with intuition to be able to enter the right markets in the right way. Even if you manage that, you must continue to reinvent your company over and over again to stay relevant.

Creating sustainability over decades is complicated. Sustainable companies have the right appreciation of luck combined with intelligent planning for an uncertain future. These companies often model themselves on successful ventures outside of their own markets. In this book, I share what I have learned both about the companies that have executed well over the long term and about those that lost sight of their goals and succumbed to panic and inertia.

SMART OR LUCKY?

It is the mark of an inexperienced man not to believe in luck.

—Joseph Conrad,
Polish-born English novelist

Chapter One

LIGHTNING DOESN'T STRIKE TWICE

What Happens When You're Lucky but Think You're Smart

Companies that were once in the right place at the right time sometimes forget that they were lucky. By taking advantage of their good fortune, they grow powerful. However, in some cases these companies focus on their power and position in the market and ignore signals that their market is changing. Because these companies take their success for granted, they do not plan for a time when an upstart will challenge them. They rely on the illusion of invulnerability as a strategy.

Lucky companies—that is, companies that find themselves in the right place at the right time—face a common dilemma. The entrepreneurs who start these companies typically understand that they are lucky; they have created an innovative product or service and brought it to market just when there happened to be a demand for their offerings. They hit the market right, and their strategy has garnered substantial rewards. However, these same entrepreneurs often lose sight of their humble beginnings and early missteps; they start to believe their own marketing hype, and they attribute their success solely to their own smarts. At this point,

1

management often begins to think that their company is invincible. Such arrogance can cause a once lucky company to falter, but this doesn't happen overnight. It may take a decade before arrogance turns an enterprise with a promising future into a dismal disaster.

This chapter presents examples of successful companies that were unable to sustain their leadership positions, explores the combination of luck and good judgment that enabled these companies to succeed in the short term, and examines the processes and practices that led to these companies' downfalls. Entrepreneurs can learn to a lot about success by studying the reasons why others fail.[1]

In the technology market, we tend to live in the moment. It is difficult to imagine a time without the Internet, a time when so much information wasn't available to so many people so quickly. Few of us remember when a single computer covered an entire city block and sold for millions. Not long ago, Microsoft was the most important emerging company in the world of high tech. Today a new batch of behemoths, with names like Google, Amazon.com, and Facebook, appear to be unstoppable. As the technology industry has grown, new companies have emerged in a steady stream and grown gargantuan and powerful. But, as I've mentioned, these companies tend to become arrogant with the growth of their revenue and influence. Sometimes they are smart enough to keep focused on their long-term strategy and the factors that brought them success, and by doing so they attain sustainability. Other times, failing to recognize that the only constant is change, they lose focus, assume their market position is permanent, and, ultimately, fail.

In the computer industry, there are many examples of companies that were lucky enough to be in the right place at the right time, but then weren't savvy enough to harness that luck in order to sustain their market position. Three particularly good examples of this pattern are Wang Laboratories, Digital Equipment Corporation, and Sun Microsystems. Each of these companies became huge and powerful by entering the market at just the right time. They were all lucky. They all had spectacular opportunities, which they took advantage of and executed brilliantly. Yet not one of these companies exists today. In 1999, Wang Laboratories sold its remaining assets to Getronics N.V., a subsidiary of the Dutch IT & Telecommunications firm KPN. In 1989, Digital Equipment Corporation was sold to Compaq Computer, Inc. (which was later purchased by Hewlett Packard). Sun Microsystems was sold to Oracle Corporation in 2009. So what happened? All three were blinded by their own hype. They began to believe that their power would sustain them into the future and that it was unnecessary to change with the times.

Why were these companies unable to sustain themselves? Let's take a look at each of them in greater depth and examine what happened that led to their downfall.

Wang Laboratories: What Happens When a Company Starts Believing Its Own Marketing

The tale of the rise and fall of Wang Laboratories is the story of a company that ultimately failed because it started believing its own marketing hype. At the center of the story is its legendary founder, An Wang.[2] He was a brilliant engineer who, at the beginning of his career, understood the importance of seizing new opportunities. What set Wang apart from other entrepreneurs of his era was the foresight to design technology that met the needs of a new market at just the right time. For example, when he founded Wang Laboratories in 1951, he focused on one of the most important needs of the nascent computer industry: core memory. He had some early luck: IBM needed his core memory invention for its new electronic calculating machine. With IBM's cash in hand, again Wang showed the same foresight by smartly moving to the next area of innovation: automating control systems that were used by companies producing machine tools. Once again, an industry leader, this time in control systems, licensed the technology that Wang designed.

But Wang had bigger plans than to simply be a supplier of parts to big industry players. He wanted to build a company that would be a power in its own right. To do this, Wang had to find a new market where he could create his own products, rather than sticking with a market that had launched Wang Labs. Wang had the vision to select a new market—automated typesetting. Although Wang's great expertise in engineering allowed him to build a product, he didn't have the money to self fund this ambitious effort and so he partnered with an industry leader, Compugraphic. This partnership taught Wang some painful lessons. Wang's agreement with Compugraphic provided cash to fund the fledgling company, but it came at a huge price. Although Compugraphic paid Wang $30,000 for each machine that Wang built, Compugraphic owned the exclusive rights to build these systems. In essence, it was the same type of deal Wang had with both of his previous ventures.

Again, Wang was not satisfied. This arrangement meant that Wang's engineering talent was leveraged for another company's gain. Not ready to give up, Wang moved forward again. As the 1960s dawned, Wang applied his engineering expertise to yet another technology revolution—the programmable calculator. Power once reserved only for hugely expensive mainframes was now available on a scientist's or engineer's desk. This was revolutionary, and it was not surprising when the desktop calculators that Wang designed began to dominate the market. At last Wang was able to escape the shadow of being a supplier of components to big industry players. This was the opportunity Wang had been waiting for. To prepare for the growth he craved, Wang took his company public on the New York Stock Exchange in 1967. The offering was hugely successful and enabled the fledgling company to expand outside of the United States, opening sales, service, and administrative offices in North America, Europe, and Asia.

At this time in the company's history, Dr. Wang used the same intuition that had led him to abandon both the control systems market and the programmable calculator market. He recognized that both of these markets were becoming too competitive.[3] Big companies with lots of money were entering these markets and would be able to commoditize them. It was time for Wang to seek out the next frontier. Rather than starting from scratch as he had done before, in 1970 Wang purchased a company with programming experience and used that experience and knowledge to enter the computer industry. Initially, Wang struggled to create a valuable computer system, but finally did so with its fourth computer, the 2200, which was designed to address the needs of companies that couldn't afford or manage a mainframe computer. The new computer fit into the hottest emerging market, the minicomputer.

This was a tough market, with big players like IBM and HP breathing down Wang's neck. But Wang ingeniously combined his phototypesetting experience with word processing capability. This was a time, when, if someone wanted to do word processing, he or she needed to know how to program a computer, so most businesses still relied on typewriters. By the mid-1970s, Wang Labs made two immensely important innovations to the computer: it added a visual display, and it turned its general-purpose computer into a dedicated word processing system. These innovations solved critical problems for business customers who wanted to automate their word processing tasks. It was the right solution at the right time.

The company was smart enough to recognize that it had a surefire hit and invested significantly in marketing. While this marketing achieved Wang's objective of positioning the company as a leader, it also sowed the seeds of its downfall. Wang was positioning itself not just as a leader that could solve customers' word processing problems, but also as the leader for the future. At this stage in the company's evolution, its aggressive marketing paid huge dividends. In fact, in 1978, even though it was only the thirty-second largest computer company, it spent almost as much as IBM did on television advertising, creating a persona that was bigger and bolder than its customer base or revenue justified. Wang cleverly presented itself to the world as a powerful company with pragmatic business technology. In one of its most memorable advertising campaigns, Wang proclaimed that, even though it was much smaller, the company was "gunning" for IBM. A bold approach to a wide-open frontier. It was also a careless move. Although Wang was clearly an increasingly important company, it did not have the same breadth of technology as competitors like IBM and Digital. In positioning itself as a market leader well beyond its capability, management began to internalize its marketing message. This is a dangerous approach for any emerging company.

It was even more dangerous because the marketing strategy was incredibly effective and Wang became well known in the market. Armed with its newfound market position and strength, the company did what many companies in this position do: it made acquisitions to increase the size and scope of its offerings. These included InteCom, Graphic Systems, Informatics Legal Systems, and minority interests in U.S. Satellite Systems and Telnova. Although large IT departments shunned these new systems, business units flocked to the company—bypassing IT altogether. They purchased Wang word processing systems because these systems got the job done better than larger, more complicated, and more expensive systems. And the company didn't stop with dedicated word processing systems. As Wang's market share in word processing systems grew, so did the number of its competitors. Hundreds of companies offered similar capabilities. Although Wang may not have viewed these companies as a threat, the company did expand the capabilities of its systems. However, unlike in previous decades, when Wang had moved boldly to change its strategy as markets changed, the company now focused only on holding on to its market share. To that end, the company supplemented its systems with the ability to manage data processing on its minicomputers. Now, business units that were comfortable with Wang word processing could use the same platform to add databases and computing. In essence, Wang developed a new market space, called the integrated information system, that was precisely what business users needed. For the next several years, Wang was able to leverage its strong position with customers who depended on its word processing systems.

During this period, the company's revenue and scope of business exploded. The company grew at an average of 61 percent a year. The fact that their systems could do both data and word processing was a big advantage and helped differentiate the company from its competitors. Today, this sounds like a simple feat to accomplish. After all, computing of words or data couldn't be all that different. However, at the time that Wang entered the market, this was a competitive advantage, and addressing this customer need paid off. By 1983, almost half of the company's revenue came from Fortune 500 companies.

By 1982, Wang reached $1 billion in sales and doubled that two years later. But beneath the veneer of success there were signs of trouble. The company was no longer as disciplined and focused as it had been in its early days. The management team grew complacent and arrogant—more driven by individual goals than by corporate goals. The marketing department became the source of "the truth." The industry was changing, but Wang didn't seem to notice. New players were entering the market. Companies that had simply purchased truckloads of new Wang systems every year now turned their attention to PCs. PCs began flooding into the same departments that had depended on Wang's unique combination of word and data processing. PCs from IBM were available with software from Microsoft. They were less expensive than Wang's minicomputers. For Wang, it was the beginning of the end.

Wang continued to spend money on marketing at the rate of an IBM, although it was much smaller. Even when it became clear that the company was losing money and market share, it clung to the belief that its size and revenue would be enough to lead it into the future. Even in 1985, when the high-flying company's revenue decreased by 66 percent and 5 percent of the workforce was laid off, Wang's management was still not convinced that they faced a long-term problem. They continued to believe that they would remain an industry leader. As the 1980s waned, Wang's revenue was more than $3 billion. Although it introduced its own personal computer and other software offerings, these could not stop the company's slide. Making matters worse, customers were now interested in the emergence of computing platforms that weren't dominated by a single vendor. An environment called Unix, based on an operating system developed by AT&T that was becoming prevalent with a myriad of startups, was also challenging Wang's market position. Dr. Wang and his team refused to recognize that the market was changing and continued to assume that their traditional products would prevail in the long term.

A company like Wang Laboratories doesn't die in a day. It is a slow-motion process that includes missteps, overreaching, misreading of the market, arrogance, and fear. In 1992, the company filed for bankruptcy protection.[4] Had Wang paid attention to new competitors and moved quickly to create new strategies and introduce different products based on where customers were headed, the company might have survived.

Here are the three key mistakes that Wang made that ultimately led to its demise:

Mistake One: Arrogance. It is ironic, but, in Wang's early years, the company survived and ultimately thrived because it was willing to learn from its mistakes, take risks on innovations, and even walk away from its most successful product, the desktop calculator, to move to the future.[5] But standing still is never an option. Once Wang became a billion-dollar company, it lost its focus. It clearly had a great marketing team and marketed itself as IBM's biggest competitor. Ultimately, it became obsessed with competing directly with IBM, not only in word processing—its key market advantage—but in data processing as well. The company's management team grew arrogant and started to view its marketing department as the source of truth rather than as the personnel responsible for positioning products. Management began to believe that it was the most powerful company in the computer market; *surely,* they reasoned, *our innovation in minicomputers and integrated word and data management, our development of broadband communications, and our favorable name recognition position us for primacy in the market.* Because of that belief, Wang spent more than it was really able to on marketing. Even when the company was losing money and market share, it continued to believe that size and revenue would be enough to sustain it.

Mistake Two: Blindness to market realities. Wang Laboratories, like its competitors, had its own proprietary hardware, operating system, and software. This was the normal way computing was then done. But in the late 1980s the market was changing. Microsoft was continuing to build its dominance as a de facto standard computing platform at the low end. At the high end of the market, the Unix operating system and open standards were starting to gain customers' attention. Expensive integrated hardware-software systems were no longer as attractive as they had been a couple of years earlier. However, unlike in Wang's early days, when it was willing to take the risk of moving to the next frontier, now company management refused to change. It decided to stick with its existing offerings long after the market had moved on. When the company finally decided that it had no choice but to change, it was too late.

Mistake Three: Assuming that market share is enough. In the late '80s, Wang's revenue was more than $3 billion. However, the company was losing market share and profits were sliding quickly. Yet the company continued to proclaim that the emerging companies that were starting to take away market share were not a threat, because the company was bigger than the upstarts.

Wang Laboratories had been well positioned at just the time when business units of large companies were looking for a pragmatic and affordable alternative to the mainframe computer. And Wang had great intuition to know when to transform his fledgling company into new markets at the right inflection point. However, as his most successful endeavor expanded, his company focused more on holding onto an incumbent position rather than innovating in a changing market, and this eventually led to Wang's downfall.

DIGITAL EQUIPMENT CORPORATION: SOMETIMES THE SMARTEST KID ON THE BLOCK LOSES

Like Wang Laboratories, Digital Equipment Corporation got its start in the 1950s and innovated in a market dominated by mainframe computers that were complex and difficult to use and manage. Ken Olsen, the founder of Digital, innovated to create a more interactive and customer-friendly computer complete with a display.[6] It wasn't clear in the early 1960s, but this was the birth of the minicomputer market—and it was revolutionary. Companies could now buy a computer for around $100,000, instead of spending more than a million dollars for a comparable product. Bigger and better-funded companies, like General Electric and

RCA, had failed miserably in the computer industry. What it took to leapfrog the industry was a bold startup that could leverage experimental computers out of MIT.

Digital broke the mold of conventional wisdom at the time. When Digital came to market, almost all computers were leased, but Digital decided to sell its computers instead. This was not an isolated decision; rather, it was the philosophy of the startup. The new company's strategy was to succeed by fostering innovation and setting up a management structure that encouraged the free flow of ideas. Any engineer with an innovative idea was allowed to pursue that dream. Up until this point, most computer companies had followed the traditional product engineering disciplines common in industrial manufacturing. Therefore, Digital Equipment's more entrepreneurial approach to product creation was a radical departure from the norm.

The company's biggest breakthrough was the PDP-8 computer. It was the right product at the right time in the market. Businesses were hungry for a computer that was inexpensive and allowed them to harness computer power at a fraction of the cost of the mainframe computer, which continued to dominate the market. Although no company was going to be able to unplug its powerful mainframe systems, what they needed was a front-end system that could be integrated into their mainframes. Digital hit the market just right. By pricing the PDP-8 at only $18,000 for a sophisticated and powerful system, Digital took the market by storm, selling nearly fifty thousand units in its first year. It wasn't just individual business units that bought the systems; vendors that packaged business software onto systems found the pricing irresistible. Inevitably, Digital attracted a new type of customer—companies that would buy the systems, package them with their own software, and resell them to small and medium-sized businesses. But Digital's bigger success came with the follow-on to the PDP-8, the PDP-11.[7]

Introduced in 1970, the PDP-11 marked a turning point for the minicomputer market and for Digital. Not only did the PDP-11 include powerful advances in computing engineering, but it also could be manufactured easily by less-skilled technicians. Therefore it became the Model T of the computer era. Selling the PDP-11 for just $10,800, the company sold six hundred thousand units. Digital followed up on this successful model with one of the most significant minicomputers in the market, the VAX-11, announced in 1977. The VAX-11 was a much more high-end system—a "super mini-computer" intended to bring Digital close to the mainframe market. Thus Digital could compete against much more expensive mainframe systems and still make a significant profit. Over the life of the company, it sold four hundred thousand of these systems.

The success of these minicomputers was both a blessing and a curse for Digital as it continued to grow. The company was indeed at the right place at the right time. However, rather than continuing to innovate, as it had done with the movement from the PDP-8 to the 11, the company's attitude toward innovation began to change. It was hardly noticeable at first, but this attitude shift had a major impact in the early 1980s, when Digital, like Wang, showed reluctance to enter the PC market. IBM had already announced its successful PC, and conventional wisdom at the time was that Digital—the company that had virtually invented the minicomputer market—would once again lead. Unfortunately, internal factions within Digital disputed just how the company should respond to the PC, and rather than base the architecture on new engineering principles, it simply repurposed the trusty PDP-8. The result was an unfocused and less-than-impressive entry into the market, with a lackluster set of PCs. At the same time, more than a hundred competing minicomputer companies were challenging Digital's leadership in minicomputers.

Like many hardware companies, Digital invested heavily in software. And like many hardware companies, it did not understand how to build sustainability in software. What transpired is ironic and tragic. If you look at the areas in which Digital innovated in software, the list is impressive, even by today's standards of software innovation. The company, for example, had innovative database products (which it sold off to Oracle); it had a product called Notes, similar to Lotus Notes, that was used internally by developers. Its proprietary operating system, VMS, was the foundation of Microsoft's NT operating system, which evolved into Microsoft's current server offerings. Digital even had an innovative office system called All-in-1. And there were hundreds of other innovations in workload automation, business rules, knowledge management, and more.[8]

Unfortunately, Digital didn't truly understand the value of software. The economics of hardware and software are very different, and Digital was primarily a hardware company. A company spends a lot of money up front developing hardware. However, once the platform is released into the market and it is at the right price point and functionality for the market, revenue comes quickly. With software, the sequence is just the reverse. The initial investment, although large, isn't as big as the investment for hardware, but revenue flows in more slowly. Customers want to try a product before they buy it. They want time to evaluate and test the software. So revenue may not start flowing for a year. However, once the software proves to meet the needs of customers, revenue keeps coming for a long, long time. The up-front expense in software development pays huge dividends for years. The incremental costs are small, but if a company has been used to enjoying the immediate revenue from hardware, the transition to a software model is painful. Digital's inability to recognize the long-term value of software led to its eventual demise.

In the end, Digital tried to revive itself by coming out with new hardware. Digital launched its ambitious Alpha processor in 1991, to a room filled with company executives, press, customers, and industry analysts. But it was too little, too late. Although the characteristics of the new hardware were impressive, it was clear that the system would not ship for at least eighteen months, and the company had nothing to sell in the meantime. Digital was paying scant attention to software, because the revenue model was uncertain compared to hardware revenue. In addition, Digital was convinced that it had to remain with its proprietary hardware and operating system. The road ahead was uncertain—and in January 1998 Digital was sold to Compaq for $9.6 billion.

Like Wang, Digital made fatal mistakes. Here are the three most significant:

Mistake One: Arrogantly assuming that great engineering trumps everything else. There is no question that Digital was a great engineering company. It innovated at almost all levels. For example, its hardware was well designed and executed. Its operating systems were well ahead of the market. Even though Digital never considered itself a true software company, it developed innovative software that, in some cases, proved to be years ahead of the market. Great engineering is a prerequisite for success. Without it, the marketplace will punish you without mercy. However, a company has to provide the right level of innovation to meet customers' needs, and Digital never did that. There was no planning based on customers' greatest problems; instead, the company simply assumed that if customers appreciated the amount of engineering sophistication built into its products, they would buy. In the end, Digital continued to innovate its engineering, but customers stopped paying attention because the company didn't innovate with the customers in mind.

Mistake Two: Ignoring market changes. As the market began to shift toward openness and standards, Digital continued to do things its own way. It assumed that the level of engineering and technical sophistication of its own operating system would always be compelling. Therefore, while Digital's competitors moved to provide Unix as an option and introduced more advanced chip technology called RISC, Digital stayed with its existing approaches. When PCs became popular, Digital assumed that, from an engineering perspective, PCs simply wouldn't make the grade. Digital offered an underpowered set of offerings and gained no momentum. It could have offered sophisticated offerings to its loyal customer base, but missed an important opportunity.

Mistake Three: Believing that size matters above all else. Size does matter, of course, but not in and of itself. Digital acted like a winner even when it wasn't winning. It acted as though its size and power made it unstoppable. Nothing is more emblematic of this lack of insight than the last huge customer meeting the company held in 1989. It was the largest customer conference in the company's history. The meeting was so large that Digital rented the *Queen Elizabeth II* to entertain its best customers. The conference was a showcase for the company's latest products and innovation. Such a massive and expensive event was clearly designed to impress. But the event also revealed underlying problems in execution of new products and the inability to hold onto existing customers. In a sense, Digital substituted a massive marketing event for a well-executed marketing and product strategy. Digital may have been showcasing impressive technology, but their execution was not relevant to their consumer base. Size matters—but only if it is combined with brilliant execution. Regardless of how big or small a company you are, first and foremost you must meet your customers' needs. Digital needed to stay focused on—indeed, even obsessed with—the changing computing landscape. Instead, the company rested on its laurels and its size. In the end, Digital couldn't sustain its competitive advantage in the market. Neither its size nor its brilliance in engineering were enough to keep profits flowing. The sale to Compaq followed, and by 1998, Digital was history.

Digital's demise resulted from arrogance, blindness to market change, and failure to remain focused on its key strengths. Had Digital's management team adapted to changing market conditions, it could have leveraged its strong brand into the new century.

SUN MICROSYSTEMS: WHY DEFT EXECUTION IS AS IMPORTANT AS A GREAT VISION

Like both Wang and Digital, Sun Microsystems was lucky; the company provided precisely the right type of products to fill a current market need. Unlike both Wang and Digital, Sun Microsystems used a standard operating systems platform to propel itself to the forefront of a new industry and leapfrog its competition. Sun's vision was based on a belief that the network of computers, not the individual computer itself, provided value to customers. Although both Wang and Digital had invested in networking technology, their focus had been around networking those computers within the four walls of a company. Sun took that vision a step further by recognizing that computing could be linked across the world. "The network is the computer" was the company's clarion call.[9]

The company was founded in 1982 by Stanford University students who had designed a new generation of computers called "workstations." Unlike the PC, the workstation offered a new level of power, integrated networking, and high-resolution graphics. The PC was perfect for the individual business user; the workstation was intended for the power user such as an engineer, scientist, or animator. Because the system was built by Stanford student Andreas

Bechtolsheim without financing, Sun used as many off-the-shelf components as possible. For example, instead of taking the years required to build an operating system from scratch, Bechtolsheim selected the Unix operating system, widely used because it was freely available for research purposes.

AT&T owned the Unix operating system and relied on it as the foundation for its network, but antimonopoly regulations prohibited the company from entering the computer business. However, the company needed its operating system in order to continue developing its communications software. As part of the agreement with the U.S. government, it was required to freely license this technology to both commercial companies and academic institutions. Because of this, Unix was widely used by engineers and scientists across the market—and especially at research universities across the world. In addition to the fact that it was freely available, it also had important technical capabilities, including the ability to execute more than one task at the same time.

Bechtolsheim called his new workstation Sun 1 (Stanford University Network) and began selling it for $10,000. Within a year of Sun's founding, several other Stanford graduates joined Bechtolsheim. The strategy of using off-the-shelf hardware and software propelled the company into a leadership position. In fact, Sun's biggest competitor in the workstation market, Apollo Computer, had actually come to market a year earlier than Sun. Many observers in the market considered Apollo's architecture and operating system to be more sophisticated than Sun's. However, the fact that Sun based its workstation on a mature and proven operating system was a lucky move that in the end served Sun much better than Apollo's elegant but proprietary approach. Sun's platform was much more accessible to partners that were also using the Unix operating system. Therefore, if a customer wanted software for the Sun platform, it was more likely to be available. In contrast, Apollo had designed its own version of an operating system, which had many of the components of Unix but included many additional features.[10] It was much more difficult and costly to move new software onto the Apollo environment.

Recognizing the benefits the company gained by using an open systems operating system like Unix, Sun decided to use its luck to further its goals in the market. The decision to use the Unix operating system was not a brilliant strategic decision in 1982; it was simply a pragmatic and lucky move based on the need to get to market without spending a lot of money. Now Sun's management team got smart. Leveraging the benefits of the Unix decision, the company decided to make open systems a strategic marketing advantage. One of the most important early moves the company made was to broadly license the product that differentiated Sun from its competitors: a distributed file system called the Network File System (NFS). NFS was originally designed to enable Sun work-stations to share data across the network, and it was one of the primary selling points for the Sun sales force. In 1984, Sun suddenly decided that it would begin licensing NFS without cost to any company that wanted to use it. Today this practice is commonplace. Most software companies not only will license their key innovations, but also will often offer a free version of the software in order to popularize it in the market and turn it into a standard that all programmers will use. In 1984 this was an innovative strategy, and it had an immediate impact. Apollo Computer had relished compet-ing against NFS with its own distributed file system but when Sun decided to broadly license its own software, NFS was transformed almost overnight into the market standard.[11]

Sun's licensing of NFS and the dramatic rise in the importance of standards and open systems propelled Sun into a leadership position in the market. Over the next three years, the company grew at an annual rate of 145 percent. By 1988, Sun was a billion-dollar company—only six years after the company was formed. In contrast, eBay—one of the Internet's greatest commercial success stories—did not reach a billion dollars in revenue until its seventh year of operation.

The billion-dollar marker is very important in the technology sector. It means that the company is well established and has significant momentum. It also means that the company isn't in danger of disappearing overnight. Now Sun was the leader in the growing workstation market. Increasingly, software companies began building their applications to support the Sun hardware and operating system platform. The growing power of Sun meant that it had the money to buy competitors. It purchased a myriad of companies to cement its dominance in the Unix operating system market. It also began to license its operating system to run on other companies' hardware platforms.

The first ten years of Sun's history were far and away the most lucrative.[12] The company grew quickly, gained market share, and dominated the market for Unix workstations. But the market was starting to change. Other market leaders, sensing that Unix was growing, began investing in the market. IBM, Apple, Compaq, and Digital Equipment entered the market in force. At the same time, Microsoft and its partner Intel were making important inroads into the enterprise computing market. So, in addition to focusing on its Unix competitors, Sun's leaders also set their sights on challenging Microsoft. Just as Sun had gained traction because Unix was so important in the scientific and engineering market, Microsoft was convincing business leaders that its own platform could support their broad needs. Microsoft had developed a significant set of partners that supported its platform. Sun believed that if it ignored and challenged Microsoft it could convince customers to change their loyalty. But battling Microsoft became a challenging and frustrating strategy that never succeeded.[13]

Sun thought of itself as a hardware company, and clearly its entry into the market—the Sun1 workstation—was a market leader. It is typical for companies that have a huge hit, as Sun did with Sun1, to have difficulty replicating that success. But Sun was persistent, both developing new hardware and buying hardware companies such as Cray, one of the pioneers in high-end systems. Sun also recognized that it would need to move up market in order to sustain its leadership in workstations, and in 1995 the company introduced high-end systems priced at more than $500,000.

Unfortunately, even as Microsoft began to gain power in the market, Sun's leaders were hesitant to embrace PCs. The growth of the PC market, and Sun's inability to embrace market changes, hurt the company. It fought against Microsoft and other companies that were beginning to change the dynamics of computing. Sun's vision for computing was compelling—the network is the computer. In essence, it posited that with a series of computers ranging from low-end workstations to high-end systems, supporting all the same software and the same connectivity, computing would be seamless.

But hardware alone would prove to be not enough to sustain Sun in the long run. Without software, it is hard to differentiate systems. In fact, in its early days, Sun focused on building systems software like its Network File System, and on ensuring that the software elements such as the operating system made the overall system work well. It was that early foray into software that helped the company grow. However, Sun was never comfortable with software as a market unto itself. The most important example of Sun's inability to embrace the commercial value of software was Java, a programming language that was developed by Sun in the 1990s. Initially, it was intended to be a consumer programming platform for the television market. However, Sun's engineering team began to see that the programming language had great potential in the emerging commercial Internet and had the vision to release it into the market. Java took off quickly and evolved into an important standard for companies across the globe. Sun had something hot. The potential for growth was huge, but unfortunately, Sun was never able to find a way to capitalize on Java.

Sun did understand that it needed software to propel itself to the next level. It began buying small, innovative software companies that had great technology but little revenue. Sun determined that, with its size and scope, it could use these innovative platforms to transform itself into a solutions company.

At the same time that Sun began to purchase these companies, the dot-com era began to take shape.[14] Once again, Sun was in the right place at the right time. Its hardware was well designed and it was a market leader—especially in workstations and smaller servers. These systems were relatively cheap, and the companies that were driving the dot-com revolution bought them like they were candy. Suddenly Sun was hotter than ever. It began advertising itself as "the dot in dot com." With the focus on the dot-com market, it was much easier to focus on hardware than on software. The money was good. But while hardware market share continued to drive the company forward, there were signs of trouble. In 2001 the dot-com market, propelled by lots of irrational venture capital investment, came to a crashing halt. Companies that were funded based on the hope that somehow their crazy ideas would turn into huge revenue someday began to fail at an alarming rate. Sun had banked on these companies and their partners and customers buying Sun's hardware. And because there was little incentive to invest time and effort in software, there was no buffer when the market turned. Suddenly, it began to look like the party was over. Sure, Sun had lots of software, but the software brought in very little revenue. Its most important future product, Java, never delivered much revenue at all—especially considering how important it had become to customers.

Sun realized that it needed to take quick action to reset expectations and revitalize the company. It focused on two key fronts: (1) deepening its focus on hardware in terms of evolving its proprietary hardware architecture, and (2) purchasing companies that would add to its hardware depth. The company was also pragmatic enough to realize that it had to offer its customers products based on the Intel architectures that most software companies supported. This helped Sun begin selling lower-priced products to appeal to smaller companies. At the same time, the company began to look at areas like storage and data management—both important and growing revenue opportunities.

These moves helped in the short term, because they enabled the company to again turn a profit—albeit a small one—by 2005. But the trend didn't last. The company's CEO for more than ten years, Scott McNealy, decided to leave the presidency and bring on a former McKenzie consultant as CEO. Jonathan Schwartz, a charismatic and brilliant thinker, had a lot of interesting and bold ideas about how to bring the company back into a leadership mode. He was determined to combine Sun's important hardware platform with software. Software was the one area where Sun could not figure out how to make money, though not for lack of trying. Between 1987 and 1992, the company purchased about thirty-five software companies. Some of these companies had excellent technologies and were at the leading edge of their markets. Schwartz had a radical idea. He decided to pull a page out of the NFS playbook and take the open source route with Sun's software. He proclaimed that, from then on, all of Sun's software would be free and the company would charge for commercial support of its offerings. The idea was that customers would purchase Sun's hardware, integrated with its valuable software. There would be a highly streamlined and simple pricing model for all software.

This wasn't necessarily a bad idea. Open sourcing a company's best proprietary software does sometimes work, but timing and execution can make all the difference. When you make a move like this, you have to be lucky—as Sun had been when it open sourced NFS. It wasn't so lucky with the open sourcing of its software this time around. The problem was that Sun's hardware was becoming increasingly commoditized; when it open sourced everything, it became difficult to build revenue.

The writing was on the wall. While Sun was inching into new emerging markets such as cloud computing, its core business was under attack from heavyweight players like IBM, HP, and EMC.[15] As Sun sank deeper into the red, customers began to get nervous about the long-term viability of the company. Sun had achieved a lot. It had managed to become a $13 billion company. However, it was clear it would be hard to replace revenue lost in a competitive hardware market with software that had been essentially offered to customers at no cost. In the end, Sun was acquired by Oracle for a little more than $7 billion. Oracle viewed Sun's hardware knowledge, its cloud computing software assets, and its installed base as a way to challenge companies like IBM, HP, EMC, and Cisco.

In the end, Sun's demise can be attributed to three key mistakes:

Mistake One: Failure to adapt to industry changes. When a market begins to change, players must move fast or be left behind. In its early days, Sun Microsystems executed brilliantly. It understood the value it was creating in getting to market before competitors by leveraging mature and widely accessible technologies. However, rather than adapting as the market grew more competitive, it remained too tied to its earlier success. There is no such thing as permanent market dominance. Therefore, even when a company gains leadership in a market, there is no guarantee leadership will be sustained. Reinvention and reexamination of the changing market landscape is the only way to ensure survival. Sun did not change its strategy until it was already a distressed company. Thus when Sun began offering its software without charge, it appeared to be a desperate strategy. By the time Sun began to change, it was too late.

Mistake Two: Failure to innovate on an ongoing basis. A strategy has to be well balanced and well executed. Sun Microsystems's initial success was based on its ability to build a well-designed hardware platform that was well integrated with all the software components needed to make the system meet customer demands. However, over time Sun was not able to continue the level of innovation needed to compete. During the dot-com era Sun was able to focus on selling commodity hardware to this growing market without having to create a balanced strategy of both hardware and software. Once the company began to seriously focus on software, it was already too late. A company will falter if it does not innovate on an ongoing basis.

Mistake Three: Failure to be flexible. There is danger in becoming ideological about products. Technologists tend to be passionate about the products they have spent their lives building and nurturing. Although this is understandable and quite human, it can also cause a company to head down dangerous paths. At a certain point, companies need to part with products or technology that had once brought them fame and fortune in order to move forward. Sun Microsystems fought hard against competing operating systems such as Microsoft Windows, refusing to support it even when customers demanded that support. Refusing to pay attention to changing customer demands can often be a fatal flaw.

There is nothing so dramatic in the business world as a company's emergence out of nowhere to become a powerhouse in an important market. Although it is possible to sustain market leadership over the long run, it is a complicated and unpredictable venture. Once a market becomes competitive, many market leaders are unprepared to fight to sustain their position. Companies too often assume that their leadership will last indefinitely. When companies are on a winning path, it is easy to ignore warning signs; such complacency may lead to disaster.

I'm a great believer in luck, and I find the harder I work, the more I have of it.

—Thomas Jefferson,
third American president

Chapter Two

GAINING AND RETAINING CUSTOMERS

How to Get Customers to Adopt and Commit to Technology

One of the most difficult tasks a technology company has is to convince customers to adopt emerging technology. The most successful companies find ways to convince customers that a product is both approachable and worth the effort. At the same time, they continue to add valuable functionality to ensure long-term loyalty.

Why do some companies succeed in convincing customers to come on board quickly and seemingly effortlessly, while other companies seem to scare customers away? It has everything to do with accessibility. Companies who make their technology accessible from the outset have a huge advantage over companies who make the initial stages difficult. The companies that survive are those that are able to quickly turn prospects into customers.

But it's not that easy for a technology company to get customers hooked on its products. High-tech companies are different from consumer product companies. Consumer product companies understand that marketing and packaging are sometimes more important than what's inside the wrapper. After all, is one brand of toothpaste that different from the next?

The same cannot be said of technology. One vendor's technology may be vastly different from its competitors'. Complicated products can be hard to sell because it may take years for a customer to appreciate a technology's benefits. Technology companies tend to develop complicated products based on deep knowledge of their intellectual property. In fact, one of the reasons that so many great technologies fail to gain traction is that they are typically developed and then sold by people who are too smart for their own good! The developers focus more on the sophistication of the underlying technology than on trying to help people who need solutions to problems. I have even heard a very smart technologist state that if a prospective customer doesn't understand the value of his product, the customer doesn't deserve to own it. With that attitude, it's no wonder that technology companies typically have trouble with their sales cycles. Customers just want something that works and is also approachable and understandable.

Getting customers to adopt new technologies is hard. In fact, one of the most difficult challenges facing a technology company is getting customers to take that first step and buy. This is especially true when the company is offering an innovative technology that the customer has never seen before and no one else has tried. In this situation it is even more important that the technology be approachable. Needless to say, this isn't an easy task.

Thousands of highly sophisticated technology companies have failed simply because customers were afraid to try a new product that seemed difficult or complex. No company wants to be the first to try something new. It's more comfortable to wait until a technology is a proven success. Even those companies that are able to convince a few early adopters to take the risk almost never reach a critical mass of customers if the technology is overly complicated.

To get customers to adopt your technology, you have to make the entry seem painless and worth the investment. Companies like Microsoft, Google, and salesforce.com have done this better than many of their competitors. What do they have in common? Although their technology might not be the most elegant, it is approachable. These companies focus on engaging customers quickly, making sure users are comfortable with the product, getting partners involved, and creating long-term relationships. For example, Microsoft's software development tools often have well-designed graphical user environments, wizards, and templates that make it easy to get started. Sure, once the customer wants to move to the next level of sophistication, developers are forced to leave that nice easy graphical environment and start coding in low-level and complicated computer languages. At that stage, however, the customer is committed. Having invested money, time, and prestige in one company's products makes it painful and expensive to turn back.

What does this mean in the customer's world? Businesses do not commit to the purchase of technology lightly. Technology purchasers are judged by how well the selected technology solves a problem. Think about it this way: let's say that you are the CIO who makes the decision to purchase Product XYZ. You have, in essence, put your reputation on the line—assuring your company that buying XYZ is a wise expenditure of resources. But what happens when, after an initially positive experience with XYZ, upgrading proves to be very complicated and expensive? How comfortable are you saying to management, "I know that I recommended that we buy XYZ, but now that we've used it for a while, it isn't as good as I thought, so we need to throw it away and buy something else." More likely, you decide to make do with the technology you paid for because turning back or asking for more funding just isn't an option.

Sometimes a company can succeed even when its technology is not so approachable. This can happen when a company develops breakthrough technology. Breakthrough technology is a product that promises to solve a previously unsolvable problem. It also enables the average consumer to quickly grasp the value of the product. But the real key to capitalizing on breakthrough technology is being the first to make it approachable.

Today we take for granted that any user can pick up a computer, a tablet, or a phone and intuitively know how to use it. This was not always the case. This type of intuitive usability began with graphical software development and the invention of the graphical user interface. There was a time when it was almost impossible to create software for a graphical environment. Most tools for this process actually had to place images in a precise place on the screen's real estate. It was grueling work. There were many companies that focused on solving the problem of making graphical development easier. Microsoft finally made Windows more usable with its third release of the Windows operating system. In an attempt to win in this emerging market, hundreds of companies focused on using the Windows platform to create products to help software developers. Most of these companies focused on the PC developer. A few decided to tackle the most complex issue of creating sophisticated software by allowing programmers to use the now ubiquitous PC as the software development platform to solve complicated enterprise software development problems. One company that took aim at this market was called Visix.

VISIX: OVERLY COMPLICATED TECHNOLOGY

Visix was founded in the late 1980s, raised venture capital, landed huge agreements with large companies like Digital Equipment Corporation, formed distribution arrangements with companies across the globe, and opened offices worldwide.[1] And by 1998 the company was out of business. That Visix would succeed seemed to be a foregone conclusion . . . until it failed. There are important lessons to be learned from the early success and eventual failure of Visix.

The company's products included very sophisticated tools to help programmers more easily create complex software. Traditionally, designing this type of software would require a programmer to write thousands of lines of very intricate computer code. This type of software development is extremely time consuming, complicated, and expensive. Visix had the potential to help programmers write sophisticated programs without so much coding. Visix offered tools for creating complex business components, such as a repeatable technique for linking applications together across physically dispersed systems without having to rewrite the code.[2] It offered developers thousands of programming tools and ways of connecting components that would have been almost impossible for all but the smartest programmers to use.

A key reason for the failure of Visix was the type of customers that formed its customer base. Visix's tools appealed primarily to the most knowledgeable and sophisticated programmers that were typically employed by large financial services companies, defense manufacturers, and telecommunications companies.[3] Developers working for these companies were solving very complicated problems and were able to appreciate the sophisticated tools that Visix provided them with. These programmers also had so much prestige within their companies that they could purchase any tools they wanted. If one tool failed, they simply purchased a different one.

But what about the millions of developers who worked for more conventional companies like insurance firms and traditional manufacturers? These developers and their managers didn't have the same open checkbook or option to experiment with new technology. So Visix was simply never able to expand its customer base beyond those more advanced, leading-edge developers who could and would take a risk with new products. Sophisticated programmers were willing to invest in any technology that could be useful, even if the technology was new and risky. In fact, the riskier and more complicated the technology, the more likely it was that these developers would invest in it. But this way of thinking wasn't widely shared by the majority of Visix's potential customers. It is hard to build a sustainable company if you are serving only a small population of brave early adopters.[4] Visix wasn't smart enough to recognize that its technology was too complicated for most developers to try, so the vast majority of developers stayed away. In the end, the company and its investors gave up and Visix shut down.[5]

Visual Basic: Easy Solutions Up Front

Around the same time that Visix was founded, Microsoft began developing its own graphical development platform, called Visual Basic.[6] Microsoft combined a graphical design tool it had bought from a developer, Alan Cooper, with a language designed in 1964 that was already used by millions of developers. Although it took a few versions before Visual Basic was mature enough in terms of its ease of use and sophistication, developers flocked to the new platform. By the early 1990s Visual Basic had established itself as a dominant graphical development platform. Meanwhile, Visix had closed its doors and sold off its remaining assets.

While companies like Visix created software that was difficult to learn, Microsoft took a smarter approach with Visual Basic and made solutions easy. Because Microsoft's software was more user-friendly up front, companies and developers were willing to make the initial investment in its products. Then, when the developer inevitably had to start writing more complicated applications or code for those applications and complications arose, developers and the companies they worked for found it difficult to justify starting over again with a new product. They were committed. They had no choice but to either hire more sophisticated developers or go through the pain of learning to use the more complicated tools. Ironically, tools from competing environments may have been more effective.

But it didn't matter. The die had been cast. The initial investment had been made, and it was too costly and troublesome to start again.

CLOUD COMPUTING: CHANGING THE WAY
BUSINESSES ATTRACT CUSTOMERS

One of the most important transitions in the software market that is changing how vendors attract customers is cloud computing. With cloud computing, a customer does not have to install complex hardware or software within its own environment to begin developing an application to solve a business problem.[7] It is analogous to the difference between running your own power plant and buying power from a public or private utility.

When the cloud data center is used as a platform to run an application, it is called "software as a service." With cloud computing, the vendor provides a fully developed system that allows the customer to add specific information and processes. The customer does not have to invest much time and money to get started.

The smart cloud computing vendors are focused on creating an easily approachable interface for their products so that customers will be willing to move beyond the testing phase. As cloud computing becomes an important delivery and development platform for software, it is more critical than ever before for the vendor to get customers invested in its products quickly. Think about it this way: in the world of cloud computing, customers have the luxury of trying out a platform for a trial period, perhaps a month or two, before making any type of commitment. In fact, it is possible to try out a platform without paying any money and then to walk away, because in cloud computing, customers can purchase packaged software, development tools, and even the computing power itself in small increments.

In the traditional software model, the customer must commit very early in the process. Once the customer purchases a piece of software, the vendor can usually count on a long-term relationship. Customers understand that they are expected to pay a yearly maintenance fee to ensure that their software has the latest updates and fixes to problems, as well as access to the company's support staff.

With cloud computing, however, the contractual arrangement is different. Vendors have to work harder to retain customers and keep them from starting over with some other cloud provider that may seem better suited to their needs. With software as a service, the customer pays a monthly fee to use software accessed through the Internet. The customer doesn't buy a system to run the software. The IT department doesn't manage it. This model is very attractive to customers who just don't want to bother with the details. A software-as-a-service company must convince the customer not only to make the initial purchase but also to repeat this process every month or perhaps every year. The most successful software-as-a-service companies understand this and therefore make the early stages of working with the software as easy as possible. For example, a company called Constant Contact offers online marketing newsletter software to small businesses that want to send out regular updates and offers to customers. The software enables the customer to track which users are reading their newsletter. Constant Contact's software provides statistics about who is reading the various articles and whether or not the prospect continued to look at the company's website. In essence, it is an effective tool for managing online marketing campaigns.

But it is still software. In order to sell its offerings, Constant Contact, like other software-as-a-service vendors, offers a trial subscription. If a small business tries Constant Contact's software on a free trial basis and finds that the application is too difficult to understand or doesn't quickly meet a business need, it will never become a paying customer. An integral part of a software-as-a-service vendor's marketing strategy must be to make the customer comfortable using the software. However, even the most straight-forward software can be complicated to the uninitiated. Therefore, to ensure that it can retain trial subscribers, Constant Contact invests heavily in customer support specialists who are tasked with helping the business managers not only to get started but also to internalize the process within their companies. Once a manager is comfortable with the application, he is more likely to use it repeatedly and become a long-term customer. It isn't just a matter of getting the customer to invest; the vendor must also make sure that the customer gets so much value from the application that the customer then uses it more and relies on it more heavily. This is how companies like Constant Contact make money. For example, it might cost only a few dollars a month to transmit a newsletter to a thousand people on a mailing list. However, when that list grows to many thousands, the price goes up. The objective for these types of companies is to make the process of working with the software a part of the business development process.

Unfortunately, in the cloud environment it can be even more difficult to keep customers using your products than it is with traditional software because each time a company like salesforce .com or Constant Contact gains traction in the market, new competition can challenge that position. With cloud computing, it is relatively easy for a customer to move from one cloud vendor to the next, so holding on to customers can be challenging. For example, one salesforce.com competitor, Zoho, offers free service for a group of three users who have a limited number of prospects and customers to track. Zoho also makes it relatively simple for a customer to move to its environment—for example, by providing a tool that makes it easy for customers to transfer their customer contact information.

There are two primary ways that cloud-based companies hang onto their existing customers. First, the vendor must provide consistent and predictable service; second, the vendor must add new, compelling features that are beneficial to customers.

In the Internet and cloud world, bad news travels fast. Serious quality problems that interfere with delivering predictable service will undermine customer loyalty in a technology provider faster than anything else. At the same time, the market is very competitive. If vendors do not add new compelling services, emerging competitors can more easily lure away their customers. At the most basic level, one customer relationship management offering might seem the same as the next. If a customer uses only the most basic functions, it is easy for that customer to move to a competing vendor. However, many software-as-a-service vendors allow customers to customize the products for their own businesses. To truly take advantage of software as a service, many customers need to incorporate their business practices into the software. Obviously, there is a natural tension between buyers and sellers. If you are a buyer, you want to make sure the environment is as simple as possible so that management and portability is simple. On the other hand, if you are a seller, you want the customer to add as much process and customization as possible. Once that happens, it is much more difficult for the buyer to leave. The seller wants the buyer to have a deep and long commitment to the environment.

With the software-as-a-service model, it is imperative for sellers to ensure that customers actually use the software. In contrast, when customers purchase software outright, even though they may never buy an upgrade or even use it, the vendor still gets money up front. With software as a service, however, the vendor needs to provide a way for customers to add their own unique processes to the basic service. For example, a sales automation service will often allow the customer to add a set of company-specific sales processes. When a customer makes the software-as-a-service platform conform to its unique ways of doing business, the platform becomes a critical component in running the day-to-day business of the company.

Not all cloud computing companies are selling applications. Many sell basic computing resources or software development tools so that a customer doesn't have to purchase these systems. For example, Google has been exceedingly successful in gaining customer loyalty. Google's approach to attracting customers differs greatly from the approach of a salesforce.com or a Constant Contact. Compared to traditional software companies, Google makes it even easier for customers to use its computing resources and development tools. It starts with a very unintimidating search interface. Although search is a very powerful tool, the interface presented by Google is remarkably friendly and simple. The simplicity of the interface combined with the deep technology of the search engine has helped Google gain traction in the search market where many other companies have failed. Companies like Yahoo, which has experienced a shrinking customer base—and many others, like Inktomi and AltaVista, which no longer exist—also had good search engines but struggled to retain customers.

There are many theories about why Google has succeeded where so many others have failed. One way in which Google has managed to hold on to customers is by using its interface to make it intuitive for customers to adopt other technologies within the Google environment. For example, Google offers such options as free electronic mail, document creation/management, spreadsheets, and more. All of these products have a well-designed, intuitive interface for ease of use. Unlike its competitors, Google does not charge individuals to use its tools. Instead, it relies primarily on advertising revenue to sustain its growth.

But companies like Google, which have been both lucky and smart, will have to continue to innovate if they are to sustain their growth. Google appears to realize the challenges it faces and has started reaching out to larger corporations in the hope of replacing Microsoft as the email and office standard. To get large companies to invest in its brand, Google will have to add the kinds of capabilities, predictability, scalability, and accountability that large companies demand from their suppliers.

Sellers that can attract prospects quickly and keep them there are more likely to succeed in the long run, even when competitive threats emerge. To do this, they must assure buyers that the product or service they are selling will be easy to use and will make the buyer successful. If a solution, no matter how well designed, is intimidating, the buyer won't purchase it. Sometimes, if the solution is truly unique, the buyer may feel compelled to put up with the pain, but inevitably another vendor will soon provide solutions that are easier to use and more compelling. When that happens, luck can go right out the window.

Lessons Learned

Lesson One: Make sure that you fully explain your technology to customers so they understand what it does and its value to them. Customers will not buy what they do not understand. You should not try to impress customers with only the depth and sophistication of the technology; rather, explain how these capabilities will help solve customers' problems.

Lesson Two: Make your product as easy as possible to use up front. Ease of use trumps complexity every time. Spend as much time on ease of use as you do on the underlying sophistication. Customers will be more willing to get involved with a technology if getting started is easy. Even if customers eventually have to deal with complexity, they will be willing to do so once they commit to implementing a product.

Lesson Three: Too much complexity without a clear business benefit will lengthen your sales cycle. If you scare customers with the depth and complexity of your technology, it will take you much longer to convince them to buy your products. If you have to spend hours explaining how your technology works, you have exposed too much infrastructure to customers.

Lesson Four: Make it safe for customers to do business with you.
Customers need the assurance that, if they partner with you, they will have the tools they need to help them succeed. This means demonstrating the value of your products to solve their problems. Help customers market their success to their management.

The most complicated challenge faced by technology companies is that of convincing prospects to become customers. Typically, difficult business problems require complicated technology solutions. Making these solutions approachable can often mean the difference between success and failure.

Luck is a dividend of sweat. The more you sweat, the luckier you get.

—Ray Kroc, founder,
McDonald's Corporation

Chapter Three

YOU'RE NOT DEAD YET

How Some Companies Come Back from Near Death Experiences

One of the most difficult tasks is to resurrect a company that is failing. Companies that can overcome this type of adversity learn how to leverage their core technology and people assets. Companies that survive the near death experience often come back stronger and better than ever.

In Chapter One we talked about companies whose luck ran out after initial success. All three of the companies mentioned in that chapter—Wang, Digital, and Sun—soared to great heights, only to be brought down by their arrogance and blindness to competitive threats. The history of high tech is replete with such examples. What is less common are companies that have a near death experience but are able to remake themselves to come back just as strong, if not stronger.

Companies that come back from the brink of failure do so largely by strengthening the bonds of trust with their customers. No matter what industry they are in, companies live or die based on trust, and if a company breaks that trust too many times, customers will just walk away. Some companies in distress often make the mistake of first looking for new innovations to mitigate competitive threats. Such companies fail to realize that, if they don't repair and cement the trust relationships they have with their existing customer base, no amount of innovation will save them.

Not all companies that survive a near death experience regain their previous powerhouse status. Some survive by finding a niche in the market where they can be a big fish in a small pond. For example, Unisys, which was formed in the 1980s as a merger of IBM's biggest mainframe competitors (Sperry, Univac, and Burroughs), struggled for years and then found success in consulting and outsourcing. Novell remains in business with a focus on security and the Linux operating system. However, the company was sold in 2010 to Attachmate. Corel, once a leader in personal computing software, found its way by aggregating a large number of Microsoft competitors to form a low-end software distribution company. There are hundreds of similar examples in the technology industry. Many other companies in the same situation took a different route by merging into stronger companies. Apollo Computer, EDS, and Compaq were purchased by HP; IBM bought Cognos, Tivoli, and SPSS. Oracle purchased PeopleSoft, Sun Microsystems, BEA, and Hyperion. The list goes on.

However, some companies that were once giants in their markets but then failed have learned from their past and gone on to succeed in different areas. There are important lessons to be learned from those companies that managed to survive and thrive. IBM and Apple are two companies that almost didn't make it but managed to reinvent themselves and become powerhouses.

For more than thirty years, IBM was perhaps the most important technology company on the planet.[1] It managed to outperform all of its major competitors. However, in 1992 IBM lost $5 billion—historically the biggest loss for any American company at that time—and conventional wisdom said that the company would not survive unless it was broken up into four or five smaller companies.[2]

In the late 1970s Apple set the world on fire with its innovative personal computer. It was hip, profitable, and unique among its competitors. However, in 1985 Apple Computer reached a critical turning point. The company was faced with a forthcoming threat from Microsoft as it was bringing out its Windows platform. Steve Jobs, Apple's founder, was feuding with CEO John Sculley; in a dramatic move, Sculley fired Jobs. The company's revenues had grown to $8 billion, but profits had dropped and the company was watching its market share and its reputation as an innovator begin to ebb. It was not clear that Apple would survive the internal and external turmoil.

Both IBM and Apple managed to resurrect themselves and become huge powers in their sectors. Very few companies that experienced similar problems can say the same. There are hundreds, of companies that have been just as revered as IBM and Apple are today but didn't make it. What differentiated IBM and Apple? How does one company survive against all odds, while another dies a slow and painful death? There isn't a single, simple answer. If there were, of course, more companies might survive. There aren't even clearly discernible patterns. At Apple, its legendary founder Steve Jobs returned and pushed relentlessly to save the collapsing company. At IBM, on the other hand, a strong leader from outside the computer industry, Lou Gerstner, led the company back from the brink of disaster.[3] Other strong-willed founders—like Digital's Ken Olsen and Sun's Scott McNealy, who were as passionate about their companies as Steve Jobs was—couldn't regain the trust of their customers and save their own companies. Even when these founders brought in outside leaders, the companies still did not survive.

So what made the difference for those singular survivors? I am sure that there are many theories, but in my experience, the following are the five main factors that increase the chances for survival of a company in trouble:

- Strong, "take no prisoners" leadership
- The ability to make painful and costly short-term changes

- The ability to anticipate the future product requirements in the face of contrary conventional wisdom
- The ability to continuously ask questions and listen
- The ability to win back the trust of old customers

Of course, even if all five of these factors are present, success is not assured. Although both Apple and IBM are strong and vibrant companies today, in their dark periods no one was willing to bet on a good outcome. Luck, of course, is always a factor. Had circumstances changed just a little in one direction or another, these companies could have failed. Also, even if a company does manage to avoid the grim reaper, it needs strong focus and strong leadership if it is to move from a demoralized and dysfunctional state to one of long-term sustainability.

Almost disappearing transforms the DNA of a company. You feel it when you communicate with their leaders. They all understand that one more wrong move would have meant the end, so they are ever-vigilant and take nothing for granted. Any hint of a competitive threat must be taken seriously. It may be a simple twist of fate that some companies disappear while others live to fight another day. Some of today's most successful technology companies are run by leaders who once worked for companies that failed. For example, both John Chambers, CEO of Cisco, and Joe Tucci, CEO of EMC Corporation, were senior managers at Wang Laboratories. I suspect that the experience of helping to lead Wang has tremendously enhanced their leadership strengths.

CHANGING IBM's DNA

IBM is the most well-known resurrection story in the history of technology. The story has been told and analyzed in hundreds of articles and books. Here's my perspective: although IBM wasn't the first or only company in computing in the 1960s, they were able to leapfrog the competition at the time by really understanding customer needs and focusing on building strong customer relationships. The company was able to aggressively anticipate new emerging markets and move quickly—often ahead of key competitors. However, as the 1980s approached, companies like Digital Equipment Corporation and Wang, and hundreds of others, saw a way to penetrate the untapped need for more accessible business computing. While the profits IBM made from the mainframe computer and its software environment were huge, customers were looking for more flexibility in their platforms. However, it was difficult for IBM to contemplate introducing competitive products that might interfere with a successful and very profitable formula that had worked for so long. IBM's leadership at the time could not imagine that the old ways would no longer work—after all, they had been proven over decades.[4] Conventional wisdom held that marketing might—not innovation—allowed a company to continue to control the marketplace well into the future.

Then the inevitable began to happen. IBM started to lose money, principally because it did not change its sales and distribution model to reflect the changes in the market.[5] Ironically, although the IBM PC was the most effective business-oriented personal computer to date, IBM failed to capitalize on its market potential. The company was smart enough to understand that there was a huge opportunity in an enterprise version of the personal computer, but ultimately it didn't know how to take the PC to the next level.

IBM believed the PC would simply be an adjunct to the mainframe business and not a separate business with its own significant revenue potential. So, rather than seriously pursuing the PC market itself, IBM was happy to allow its key partners, Microsoft and Intel, to leverage their relationship with IBM to become huge powers. The problem recurred when IBM began to bring out mid-range systems and technical workstations. Also, the sales and marketing organization became fragmented, and the mainframe sales team saw the PC not as a means to increase revenue per customer but as a threat to its sales. This type of fighting between brands within the company caused massive problems.

By the end of the 1980s, IBM had devolved into a dysfunctional company, with factions fighting each other for primacy. There was no effort to cross-sell or upsell customers. Each platform group acted as though it were a separate, autonomous business. Developers designed specialized software and never collaborated across the company. It was normal to see one IBM division being undermined not by a competitor but by another division within IBM. There was no sense of solidarity within the company.

By the beginning of the 1990s, the situation had greatly deteriorated; IBM's leadership was confused and seemed to have lost its way. What business would define IBM's future? What did customers really want to buy? If you asked two different executives, you would get three different answers. As a direct consequence of this confusion, IBM became focused internally instead of on its customers.

During this period, some major failures caused by this dysfunction led to the erosion of customer trust. Naturally, all companies looking for new revenue opportunities have setbacks. But when failures come in waves, it is a symptom of serious management and organizational issues. In the case of IBM, there were at least three sequential serious product failures. Taken all together, they sent a clear message to the customer: *We can't be trusted to deliver on our promises.*

Because I lived through this era, I remember the names of these failed products very well. In fact, even today, if I want to tease a high-level IBM software executive, I just have to mention three product names—AD/Cycle, SAA, and OfficeVision—to make the executive turn white. AD/Cycle was intended to automate the programming process so that developers could avoid coding, but the implementation was too complicated for programmers to either learn or work with. Software Applications Architecture (SAA) was a major architectural revamping of IBM's entire software portfolio to create one seamless software platform that would enable customers to easily combine everything from the high-end mainframe to the person computers. OfficeVision was an office automation platform, similar to today's Microsoft Office, intended to work on all of the hardware platforms that IBM sold, ranging from the mainframe to the PC. Strategically, IBM was right to help customers better manage complexity. However, the execution of the plan was too big and too complicated—and it didn't work. OfficeVision, intended to be the first product implementation of Software Applications Architecture, was designed to provide a next-generation office productivity suite that would use the backend mainframe and mid-range systems combined with a graphical frontend based on the personal computer. Because the product had to be designed to accommodate the idiosyncrasies of each hardware platform, it didn't work well.

It boiled down to this: IBM had great customers, great sales teams, and great historical leadership in technology. But it also had a dysfunctional management team and multiple failed products, and the company was too set in its rigid political and organizational structure to implement significant changes. IBM was losing the confidence of its customers. Revenue began to drop.

At this point, IBM had only two choices: either get the company back to disciplined financial health or break IBM into a set of smaller companies. The first choice would be excruciatingly difficult, but the alternative was even worse. IBM's value to customers was based as much on the power of its brand as on the implementation of its products.[6]

The transformation of IBM took place in two phases. The first phase was intended to bring IBM back to financial stability under the leadership of Lou Gerstner, who had previously run RJR

Nabisco. Although he had been an IBM customer, he was not a technologist. He did understand fiscal discipline and the value of leveraging a strong brand in a growing market. By the time Gerstner started as CEO in 1993, the company had an $8.1 billion loss for the year. One of the primary reasons for this big loss was that customers were moving away from IBM's cash cow—the mainframe. The entire cost structure of IBM as a company was designed to support and sell this high-priced hardware.

Gerstner recognized that IBM would have to be transformed dramatically in order to survive. He brought back financial discipline. He sold off unprofitable divisions. Most important, he forced IBM's leaders to think and act differently both internally and externally. He transformed what had become a comfortable culture, filled with redundant processes and fierce internal competition, into a company focused on customers. He forced IBM leaders to think of themselves as a single company. He also achieved his most important legacy: he brought the customers back from the brink. He met with all major IBM customers and worked to bring back their trust.[7]

Gerstner was famous for saying that he wasn't worried about vision. This is because even during its period of decline, IBM wasn't standing still; in its labs it was developing a huge amount of technology that potentially could transform the company. Although it would have been easy to simply break the company up into smaller independent companies, Gerstner recognized that the IBM brand was potentially the most powerful asset that the company had. He resisted the push for fragmentation from the financial community. Instead, he focused on building one company, where business units would work to collaborate rather than to compete.

During his nine years with the company, Gerstner stabilized IBM financially and helped the company's leaders focus on new technology innovations that mattered to customers. Because of his leadership, IBM moved from basically relying on a single hardware platform for revenue and growth to focusing on hardware, software, and services. It began buying companies that would support this new strategy.

Once Gerstner had transformed IBM financially and organizationally, it was time for the next leader who could build on the new foundation. At that stage, in 2002, Gerstner handed the reins over to Sam Palmisano, a long-time IBM veteran. Now that IBM was stable, Palmisano had the luxury of focusing on customer-focused innovation.[8] Armed with a new strategy, renewed customer trust, and financial stability, it was time to take the company to the next level.

Pamisano focused his energy on creating a strategy that combined the next generation of hardware, software, and services to complement each other.[9] He made sure that the same consistent software elements were added to all of IBM's hardware platforms, so that, if customers so desired, they could run the same infrastructure elements on the mainframe or a mid-range system. On the services side, IBM purchased a series of services companies, including the business consulting arm of PriceWaterhouseCoopers. On the software side, IBM had unified all of its software products into one organization in 1995 and put Steven Mills, an IBM software executive, in charge of all software across the company. Steve Mills, now senior vice president in charge of both software and hardware, was one of the unsung heroes of IBM's transformation. Mills singlehandedly got all software business units to leverage a consistent set of underlying foundational technologies across a massive portfolio and to move to a single underlying platform. By insisting on a single set of components, he ensured that the software business units could focus on the business value of the software. As IBM purchased hundreds of software companies, it was able to transform each acquisition by putting it through the same rigorous transformation process. It was not always quick, because some acquisitions were easier to integrate than others, but it was effective.

Through a combination of luck and sophisticated sales, marketing, and customer relationships, IBM again regained its stature as a giant in computing. But it did not return to its old complacency. To this day, the company continues to purchase software companies to fill out its massive portfolio and focuses on transforming the traditional approach to business solutions by offering business process frameworks that can take the place of packaged software. At present, IBM is reenergizing its hardware business and leveraging the strength of its management team by taking the time and effort to nurture its leaders and move them across business units. It is all part of the process of remaining competitive. In 2011, IBM celebrated its one-hundredth anniversary.

Transforming Apple, Inc., from a PC Maker to a Commercial Brand

IBM managed to leapfrog the competition and quickly became successful in the highest end of the computer industry; Apple, Inc., started at the low end of the market and grew more slowly. Apple was founded in 1976 by twenty-one-year-old Steve Jobs and twenty-six-year-old Steve Wozniak. In the late 1970s, the idea of an individual owning a computer seemed absurd. In fact, personal computers were primarily used by hobbyists who enjoyed programming for fun.[10] Apple had bigger competitors like Commodore and Tandy when it introduced its first commercial computer, the Apple II. However, unlike its competitors, Apple saw itself as much as a marketing company as a technology innovator. The company hired Regis McKenna, a highly successful advertising and public relations company, to design a logo and advertising campaign. Apple differentiated its product with the addition of a color graphical screen and, even more important, with one killer application. This application made the combination of plastic, wires, and computer chips come to life. It was VisiCalc, the first computerized spreadsheet, designed and programmed by two young computer scientists, Dan Bricklin and Bob Frankston. Suddenly, anyone who needed to do analysis or what-if scenarios could combine the power of the personal computer and the spreadsheet. The combination of VisiCalc with sophisticated consumer-focused marketing propelled Apple into a leadership position in the market.[11]

By the end of 1978, Apple was one of the fastest growing companies in the United States; two years later the company went public. Despite the incredible success of the Apple II, the follow-up, the Apple III, was a disaster. Perhaps the developers were overly complacent; maybe they underestimated the challenges they faced. Whatever the case, by 1981 the company had laid off a significant number of employees and changed its management team. Mike Markkula, an industry veteran who had served as a mentor to Apple and who also had purchased a third of the company in the late 1970s, reluctantly became its president and CEO. Rather than give up, Apple increased its spending on software development.

Many companies, faced with this type of risk, push back. They curtail spending and adopt a bunker mentality. Apple took a different approach. It had already achieved some impressive objectives. By 1982, the company had sold 650,000 computers world-wide and was the first personal computer company to achieve $1 billion in sales. However, there were looming threats that would change Apple forever.

In 1981, IBM, together with its two partners, Microsoft and Intel, brought its own personal computer to market. Although Apple executives were confident that their platform was superior, the corporate market was more trusting of IBM than it was of a relatively new, small personal computer company that hadn't yet proven itself. Apple's management team hoped that the IBM PC would not take hold. However, it was worried about the potential impact on revenue. It needed something different to keep customers focused on their platform in the face of this competitive threat.

Jobs and Wozniak turned to Xerox PARC, the computer research lab run by Xerox Corporation, which employed some of the world's most brilliant and innovative computer scientists. The goal was not necessarily to create products that would sell immediately but rather to do the research that would drive future innovation. One of the most intriguing innovations was a new way to present code on a computer screen—a graphical user interface. Ironically, in 1981, when Xerox itself tried to leverage its innovative interface with a product called the Xerox Star, it was a failure. The product was elegant, but it was about ten times more expensive than other products in its category. It also lacked the networking and the partnerships it needed to create a successful business. After seeing this innovation, Apple's engineers thought they had found a differentiator that would potentially allow the company to keep ahead of IBM and its partners, so they developed a new graphical system called the Apple Lisa. It was a beautifully designed system, well suited for graphical applications like publishing. However, its appeal was too limited and the product was too expensive.

The situation at Apple continued to deteriorate. Although Markka had taken the reins of the company to help stabilize it, he had not intended to remain in the job over the long term. So in 1982 Steve Jobs convinced John Sculley, the CEO of consumer products company Pepsico, to become CEO of Apple.

Armed with the lessons of the Lisa, Apple introduced the Macintosh in 1984. It made a dramatic entry into the market with its famous Super Bowl ad.[12] The legendary ad was based on George Orwell's novel *1984,* set in a world populated by brainwashed minions (that is, IBM customers) in the thrall of a dictator intent on complete domination. Apple boldly proclaimed the end of computing as we know it. This single ad cost Apple almost $1 million.

Although the desktop publishing market appreciated the Macintosh, its platform—like the Lisa—was expensive and lacked the broad base of applications that personal computer buyers were beginning to demand. To make matters worse, there were quality problems. A power struggle for the soul of Apple ensued between Jobs and Sculley. By 1985, Jobs was forced to leave the company and immediately started a new company called NeXT, intended to leverage the graphical environment initiated by Apple but to create a more elegant operating system and software development platform.

The next several years were good for Apple. Under Sculley's leadership, the Macintosh was marketed as a corporate platform. As more applications were made available, including Microsoft's office products, the company grew. By 1988 the company had sales of more than $4 billion. [13]

But as the market for personal computers exploded, Apple's position as the leading graphical personal computing platform came under attack. Apple had made the mistake of underestimating Microsoft's ability to create its own graphical environment. Microsoft's first two versions of Windows were terribly designed and too slow to be a threat to Apple. However, Microsoft was a tenacious company that did not give up easily. By the time the third generation of Windows came to market, it was a huge threat.

Apple's reaction was to sue Microsoft and its partner Hewlett Packard for copyright infringement. A year later, Xerox Corporation sued Apple for using the Xerox technology as a foundation for the graphical interface of the Macintosh. Although Apple won its case against Xerox, it lost the Microsoft case. In essence, the court ruled that copyright protection could not be based simply on appearance; it had to be based on how the technology was programmed.

By initiating the lawsuit against Microsoft, Apple demonstrated that it was relying on its legacy rather than its ability to innovate. Losing the lawsuit came as a major shock and was an important turning point in the company's history. It was becoming clear that holding on to past innovation wasn't going to be enough and that it could no longer assume that past successes would be the ticket to future success.

Apple missed the signals in the market in part because it had become much more of a marketing company than a technology innovation company. Marketers, not technology leaders, dominated its management team. Through much of the 1990s, Apple struggled to find its way. As is typical when a company begins to lose momentum and money, it looks for quick remedies. It was clear that having a graphical user interface wasn't enough, so management decided that it would make a move for market share. It was able to increase market share in the PC market from 11 percent in 1990 to 19 percent by 1992, but had to reduce its prices to do so.[14] In 1991, earnings were down 35 percent; to stem the bleeding, Sculley cut prices by 30 percent, while increasing production of notebook systems by 60 percent. This is a typical way in which highly commoditized product companies approach a competitive market. More layoffs followed, with Sculley reducing staff by 10 percent, especially in sales, and cutting top management salaries.[15] He tried to improve the picture by reorganizing into four market segments: education, large enterprises, small business, and consumer. Each group had its own R&D organization and finance divisions.

Apple was in an awkward position. It was trying to find ways to increase its market share by offering products similar to those of its PC competitors. It was falling into the same trap that IBM did in the 1970s and 1980s when each product group acted as though it were a separate company. At the same time, Apple thought that joint ventures would help it gain legitimacy in the corporate market; it embarked on joint development ventures with IBM that produced few meaningful results. The company was losing direction.

During the early 1990s, Apple leadership began to rethink its strategy. It recognized that it needed more interesting, better developed, and more innovative products to sustain its market position, but it didn't have the leadership to realize that vision. In 1993 Sculley was replaced by Michael Spindler, who had been president of Apple Europe. Spindler believed that Apple's only hope was to license its technology and encouraged the creation of an Apple clone market—a move that simply eroded profit margins and did not help the company differentiate itself. Moving back to its core, the company introduced the PowerMac, a more powerful Macintosh built on IBM's power chip. The product was well received, but the company did not execute its go-to-market strategy effectively, and it underestimated customer demand—by $1 billion. Needless to say, Spindler was replaced by the board.

This time, in 1996, the board went to another outsider, Gil Amelio, a well-known turnaround artist. Amelio had led the recovery of one of the largest semiconductor vendors of the day, National Semiconductor. Unfortunately, he had no clear understanding of the value of Apple to its customers. He also did not understand the unique culture that made Apple different from its competitors. His response was to cut expenses dramatically. Although this approach was similar to the one taken by Gerstner at IBM, there was a clear difference. Gerstner studied the IBM culture and had an appreciation for what made the company great.[16] Amelio focused only on the finance side of the business, without paying any attention to culture or the reasons why customers were loyal to Apple. A year after he arrived, the financial loss reached $1 billion. Apple's market share fell to only 4 percent and its stock price slipped to $14. The following year, Amelio was out.

Despite his many failings, Amelio took one lucky action that probably saved the company. In 1996, Apple bought Steve Jobs' new company, NeXT, for $377 million, and the contract stipulated that Jobs would join his old company as an advisor. Thus, twelve years after his departure, Jobs returned to the company he had helped found. Shortly after the board fired Amelio, it named Jobs to the position of interim chief executive officer.

The change became apparent almost immediately. Jobs reverted to the organizational structure and culture that had made the company great in the 1980s. He eliminated the bloated management structure put in place by his successors. He also understood that the company's product strategy was too complex. He did away with the licensing agreements that had resulted in the Apple clone market. He got rid of peripheral products—such as printers, scanners, and portable digital assistants—and other products that had fared poorly in the market and had taken focus away from the company's core business: its unique brand of desktop and portable Macintosh systems. The transition was painful. With a critical need to raise cash, the company did the unthinkable—it sold stock to its archrival Microsoft.[17]

However, these actions alone would not have been enough to reenergize the company. Although sophisticated customers such as graphic artists and engineers flocked to the Macintosh and Power-Books, the company needed new platforms to broaden its appeal. In 1998, Apple introduced a successful low-end product designed for the mass market, the iMac. It might have seemed inconsequential at the time, but with it, Apple made its next step into the consumer market. Rather than sporting the traditional beige, white, or silver colors, the iMac came in blueberry, lime, tangerine, strawberry, and grape. Though this made no difference in terms of what was happening inside the box, it made these new lower-priced systems seem approachable—and even fun. The iMac was an indicator of where Apple was headed. It was appealing to a new generation of users with an approach closer to entertainment than number crunching. However, behind the pretty colors was a very sophisticated next-generation operating system that was light years ahead of what Microsoft had achieved. With this success and the company's return to profitability by the end of the decade, Jobs was now fully in charge.

Apple's next innovation was not based on inventing a brand new technology.[18] The idea of the iPod was not new; indeed, companies had been developing digital media players for years. Although many of them were competent machines capable of playing music, Apple engineers were able to leverage their knowledge to increase usability. The interface and ease of use, combined with an online music store, propelled a mass-market device into the mainstream. In addition, Apple was able to overcome the legal issues that had plagued companies like Napster, which provided a platform that allowed users to share music.

The company's chaotic years of missteps were instructive, and Apple's leadership has not looked back. Apple's stock price in 1984 was $26.00; in 2005 it ranged between $32 and $74 per share. In 2010, a share of Apple stock sells for more than $300. Apple has managed to continue to innovate with its desktop and laptop platforms, and their ease of both use and maintenance has allowed the company to keep prices high while gaining market share. With the iPod for music and video, Apple has found the right formula to innovate in the mass market. It has continued this innovation with its tablet computer, the iPad. As with the iPod, the technology behind the iPad is not new. There have been tablet computers in the market for many years, including one from Microsoft. But Apple has learned how to combine ease of use, compelling innovation, a well-constructed partnership strategy, and a unique understanding of how to combine sophisticated computing with consumer market appeal.[19]

Companies that survive after transitioning to new customer requirements are rare. Every industry is filled with examples of once-great companies that lost their way and their differentiation, only to find themselves in a hopeless death spiral. Companies that go through this process and survive and thrive are of a different breed. They understand that they were lucky to survive. These companies remain alert, vigilant, and grateful for their luck. But obviously luck alone isn't enough to account for survival. It is a total transformation and a recognition that the focus must be on where the customer is headed—not where the customer has been.

Lessons Learned

Lesson One: Realize that a focus on the company's intellectual property is necessary for survival. A company needs to get to the heart of what intellectual property is important and relevant to customers and get rid of the rest. At that point, the company can transform the portfolio of offerings with technology that will reengage customers.

Lesson Two: Regain customer trust. Once a company begins to lose sight of its customers' needs and wants, it can quickly become irrelevant. Therefore leadership must focus on retaining both customer and employee trust in order to survive.

Lesson Three: Listen carefully to what the marketplace is telling you and then take action. The market will send strong signals about what it wants and what it doesn't want. When companies are in a free fall, it is often difficult to listen to those signals. Your most important customers, those who are invested in your success and survival, will provide you with early indications of trouble. It is human nature to want to dismiss what can be harsh criticism. However, no matter how hard it is to listen to bad news, it is the first step in making meaningful change.

Lesson Four: Make strategy changes. It may be uncomfortable, but it is necessary. Companies in trouble don't like to take risks; they tend to try to copy strategies from the last generation of successful companies. Companies that are at a significant transition point need to think outside of the box by looking to the future and creating new strategies. This is much harder than it may appear.

Both IBM and Apple today are strong companies with growing stock prices and an expanding customer base. However, only a few years ago it wasn't clear that either company would survive. To survive a near death experience, a company must reinvent itself by retaining the important culture that made it great and by expanding its products, based on a keen understanding of customer needs.

I believe in luck: how else can you explain the success of those you dislike?
                              —Jean Cocteau, French poet, novelist,
                                    playwright, artist, and filmmaker

Chapter Four

THE GOOGLE SNEAK ATTACK
Supplanting the Market Leader

Sometimes when a company enters a market just at the right time, it assumes that it can supplant the existing market leaders quickly. Challenging a market incumbent before a startup establishes sufficient revenue and customer loyalty can lead to disaster. To be successful, emerging players must take a more subtle approach to achieving market leadership.

The path from creating an inventive but unrecognized concept to becoming a powerful market leader is complicated. A company armed with an interesting technology, some high-powered supporters, and a little cash can seemingly come out of nowhere and suddenly be on top of the world. These companies often are surprised when a bigger competitor notices and sets out to stop them. Occasionally the upstart withstands the onslaught. More often, the market leader succeeds in destroying the fledgling company—this is simply a fact of life in highly competitive markets. Big companies with deep pockets are used to dealing with competitive threats and have the means to do so effectively. Upstarts have fewer customers and less money, and they generally lack the resources and strategies to take on the giants. In essence, they are not mature enough to compete.

But every once in a while a company does succeed in supplanting the market leader. So why is it that some upstarts catch fire and gain huge market share, whereas others have a brief moment in the sun and then fade back into oblivion? The companies that succeed keep their eye firmly focused on the customers—both where the customers are and where they are headed. They are patient, they carefully prepare a clear strategy for where they are going, and they get the timing right. They also don't fully announce their intentions to the big companies in the market they are trying to compete against, and they certainly don't publicly declare war on a market leader. I call this a "sneak attack" strategy. A sneak attack happens when a company presents itself to the market as an organization that provides a useful technology that fits well with existing products in the market. Customers and vendors welcome the upstart because it appears to be complementary rather than threatening. In a well-designed sneak attack strategy, an upstart's large competitors shouldn't even see them as a threat until it is too late.

Netscape, Google, and Amazon all planned sneak attacks. However, while Google and Amazon succeeded on a massive scale, Netscape took on the giants too quickly and too aggressively and wasn't so lucky. Let's take a look at the stories of these three companies.

NETSCAPE: THE GIANT THAT COULD HAVE BEEN

By 1996 the Internet had been around for eleven years, but it was not yet a network for mere mortals to use. It had no graphical interface, and in order to get to a location the user had to type in the specific Internet Protocol address, which consisted of a string of digits, dots, and letters indicating where the information was stored. Then, once the user found an address, the user had to know specific commands to navigate further into the network. It is not surprising that this world was the purview of scientists and computer wizards and definitely not for the average business person.

This started to change when several organizations designed graphical browsers to make the vast Internet easier to use. The first commercial breakthrough came in 1993 when the National Center for Supercomputing Applications (NCSA), housed at the University of Illinois at Urbana-Champaign, developed a graphical interface that provided a much more intuitive way to find information on the Internet. The browser, Mosaic, was developed by Marc Andreessen and Eric Bina. Mosaic might have gone the way of other early browser initiatives and faded into oblivion, but the Mosaic developers were ushered into the commercial world when Jim Clark, a computer scientist who founded the computer company called Silicon Graphics, recruited Marc Andreessen to create a company that would commercialize the research effort. Armed with venture capital, Netscape was born in 1994.[1]

Netscape entered the market just as the dot-com boom was starting in earnest. The objective of the company was simple and compelling—level the playing field and make the Internet accessible to everyone. Although this seems obvious now, at the time it was a revolution. Suddenly, knowledge that had only been accessible to a few technologists could be distributed across the globe. In 1994, shortly after it was founded, Netscape introduced Mosaic Netscape 0.9. A month later the browser was renamed the Netscape Navigator.

Prior to the dot-com era, a typical company took years of building revenue and a strong customer base before going public. But everything was changing in the 1990s. Netscape went public in the summer of 1995, just one year after incorporating. Although the share price had initially been set at $14 per share, by the time the offering was announced it had risen to $28 per share. Netscape gained huge market traction. After only one day as a public company, shares were selling at $75. Not bad for a company with revenues of about $85 million. Netscape was off and running. In its first year as a public company, revenues doubled every quarter.[2]

Two factors set Netscape apart: it was the first graphical browser, and it worked identically on any computer. Other browsers exhibited a different appearance and behavior on different systems. Netscape designed its browser to work across operating systems, anticipating that this would be a compelling long-term differentiator. It could run on Windows, Mac, and almost all versions of Unix from the major vendors in the enterprise market including Digital Equipment Corporation, Sun Microsystems' Solaris, IBM, and Hewlett Packard.

But Netscape was an ambitious company with no intention of resting after its initial success. It began to think that this graphical browser could turn the computer industry upside down. Netscape saw the browser as becoming more important than the operating system. If the browser could make the underlying operating system—like Microsoft Windows—superfluous, Netscape could replace Microsoft as the company that would control the future of the desktop.[3]

Netscape's leaders were not the least bit subtle about their ambitions.[4] With the money made from its successful browser, Netscape began purchasing companies in multiple areas. It bought a search engine, an application server, a publishing system, a procurement engine, a retail procurement engine, an online bill payment engine, and companies in areas such as calendaring, electronic mail, meeting scheduling, instant messaging, directory services, and web page development. It even proposed to make money by selling ads on its web page. A decade later, Google was able to use the advertising model to become a market leader.

Netscape had a hugely successful initial public offering (IPO)—one of the biggest that the market had ever seen. The company came out of nowhere to completely dominate the browser market. Management looked into the future and began to believe it was possible to make the operating system irrelevant. What if it no longer mattered to customers what operating system was running on the hardware they purchased? What if software companies could write their applications to the Netscape browser rather than to a

Microsoft operating system? In essence, the power in the market would shift in Netscape's favor.

However, storm clouds were just over the horizon. Because Netscape was growing so quickly, it was beginning to have quality control problems, and worse, there were many established companies that were not pleased with Netscape's power grab. The company that had the most to lose was, of course, Microsoft. Because Microsoft dominated the desktop software market with a 90-percent market share, it was not particularly interested in the browser market in the early 1990s, when Netscape was gathering momentum. In fact, Microsoft had resisted coming out with its own offerings for the Internet. However, because of the overwhelming popularity of the Netscape browser and the company's not-so-subtle approach to the market, Netscape caught Microsoft's attention. Microsoft had no intention of letting Netscape steal its position as a market leader.[5]

Microsoft came out swinging. The company launched its own browser, Internet Explorer, based on the same base technology that Netscape used. Initially, Internet Explorer was no match for Netscape, but a company as big and powerful as Microsoft would not willingly cede control of desktop computing to a much smaller company. One of the characteristics of a market leader is the patience to focus on a goal without flinching. This is precisely what Microsoft did. First, Microsoft began to turn the browser from a revenue source into a commodity. Given Microsoft's revenue stream from the Windows operating system, it could well afford to give away the browser as part of the platform. It took three years for Microsoft to match Netscape's functionality, but with the announcement of Explorer 4.0, it was actually able to surpass Netscape in functionality, not just match it. With its browser tied to the Windows operating system, Microsoft was able to convince its hardware partners to start using Explorer as the standard. Microsoft's frontal assault, combined with Netscape's quality problems, caused Netscape to lose its momentum and its position in the market.[6]

Was Netscape smart to have attacked Microsoft directly? It was clearly a huge gamble, born out of the tremendous success of its IPO. Netscape's management team became arrogant and sloppy and also made it too obvious that it was gunning for Microsoft. I remember very clearly a meeting I had in the late 1990s, after Netscape was no longer an independent company, when I posed this question to Steve Ballmer, Microsoft's president at the time: if Netscape hadn't taken on Microsoft so aggressively, would Microsoft have partnered with the company? His very interesting answer: Microsoft was always going to invest aggressively in the browser market, but had Netscape not been so aggressive, Microsoft would have been more careful in its approach to the competitive threat.

Microsoft took on Netscape with a vengeance. It simply had no intention of allowing a tiny and lucky company to devalue the Windows operating system. The company's answer to Netscape came quickly, with the introduction of Internet Explorer as a free component of the Windows operating system. It was war—the most powerful client-based operating system company on the planet launching a full retaliation on the lucky startup that had presumed to take it on. Although Netscape worked valiantly to add more and more features to its browser, it simply could not match Microsoft's money and clout in the market. Microsoft could offer Internet Explorer as a free component of Microsoft Windows, and no matter what new functions Netscape introduced, it could not compete with a free offering. Netscape's core revenue stream eroded. By the end of 1997 the company had its first loss of $115 million. By 1998 layoffs began, but it was already too late. By the end of that year the company was sold to AOL (America Online).[7]

Netscape failed because it lost sight of its good fortune and started acting as though it were a much stronger company than it actually was. It assumed that because of the scale and speed of its initial success it was strong enough to seize dominance from Microsoft. Netscape did not employ the kind of sneak attack strategy necessary when taking on a company with the market clout, money, and aggressiveness of Microsoft. Rather, Netscape launched a frontal attack without a smart long-term strategy. Its luck could not last forever. The end of the Netscape story might have been happier if Netscape had stayed under the radar and partnered with Microsoft and other market leaders. Or if it had looked beyond the Microsoft computing model to a model that was a generation removed, it might have taken Microsoft longer to respond. But as it was, the results were inevitable.

THE GOOGLE SNEAK ATTACK

Like Netscape, Google came to market out of obscurity. Netscape was lucky because it was the first company to commercialize the Internet with the browser; Google entered an already established market—the search engine market.[8] Companies like AltaVista, Yahoo, Inktomi, and dozens of others were well known to customers. Search engines were revolutionizing how people could find what they were looking for across the World Wide Web of data. At first glance, Google's differentiation was subtle.[9] The search engine didn't seem all that different from those of its competitors, but it actually took a different approach to searching. AltaVista focused on the speed with which a customer could search, Yahoo focused on providing a complicated set of links and navigations, and Inktomi sold its engine only to service providers. Google sold its search engine to service providers as well, but it also offered it directly to consumers. The real difference between Google and its competitors, however, was the sophistication of the mathematics of its search engine. Traditional search engines focused on creating massive indices and matching important words. Although this process worked well in the early days of the Internet and Internet searching, it was too slow and cumbersome when traffic on the web exploded in the twenty-first century. In contrast, the concept behind Google search is based on ranking web pages.[10] This means that the search engine looks for how often pages on the web are viewed and which links on those pages are most frequently accessed.

In some ways, however, the starting points of Netscape and Google were not that different. Both companies took an under-appreciated Internet resource and transformed it in unanticipated ways. Both companies had huge aspirations for achieving incredible power and turning the world upside down. But the approaches that each company took, and the resulting outcomes, were dramatically different.[11]

Whereas Netscape relied on revenue from its products, Google assumed that it would get its revenue from advertising. Netscape had a traditional software company revenue model; Google was a media company, so from the beginning it was able to use a different approach to the market. Not that Google ever proclaimed to the market that it was a media company; to the average market observer, Google looked like a software company.[12] It offered products as a software company would, but it acted differently. Its sneak attack was to build a long-term strategy based on a financial model that allowed it to give products away while building a powerful media empire. Remember, a sneak attack means flying under the radar, not revealing one's true strategy and objectives. If Google had come to market not as just another search engine but as a media company that intended to become a powerhouse driving billions in advertising revenue, it would have attracted attention. I suspect that there would have been a major assault on the fledgling company and it might not have survived. But Google was much more subtle.

Like Netscape, Google was founded by students from Stanford University, Larry Page and Sergey Brin, who had worked on the Stanford Digital Library Project, a National Science Foundation founded project intended to create the technology to support a universal digital library. Based on this research, the two computer scientists registered the Internet domain site, Google.com, in

September 1997; a year later Google became a company.[13] After incorporating, the young company received $100,000 from another entrepreneur, Andy Bechtolsheim, a cofounder of Sun Microsystems. Page and Brin had ambitions of becoming an important company, so they needed capital to expand quickly. Accordingly, they raised $25 million in venture capital. Then in 2004 the young company went public and raised an astounding $1.6 billion.

From the outside, Google looked like a traditional search engine, though customers and technologists alike found it more useful and easier to use than competing offerings. However, unlike its competitors, Google never saw itself as competing in the search engine market. The search engine provided Google with an important launch point, without causing competitors to become nervous. First, it focused on several factors within the search engine that were different from its competitors. These included impressive processing speed and a well-designed search algorithm that did a better job of understanding the context of what someone was searching for. But this was just the tip of the iceberg. In fact, as Google began to compete in the market, its great advantage was the simplicity of its design. Unlike competitors such as Yahoo, the Google interface was simple and clean. It was not intimidating to the novice who just wanted to ask a question, but even the most jaded computer geek could access advanced search functions in the environment. Therefore, the value of the Google model was the design of its webpage. With a clear and simple design, Google did not annoy or intimidate the user.[14] If users wanted to see a complex set of options, it would be their choice, not the search environment's choice. Getting the user comfortable at the outset makes it much easier to hold on to that customer.

But Google's most important innovation was the business model itself. Google was lucky enough to come to market after Netscape had failed. Netscape had charged consumers $60 to buy a license for its Internet browser, which brought huge revenues into the company's coffers. However, as soon as Microsoft began giving away its browser, the game was over. Google avoided this trap by not charging for its search engine. As for its advertising model, Google took the same approach as it did with the search engine. It adopted a style of advertising that was unobtrusive and inoffensive. Unlike the interface chosen by some competitors, Google's ads were not placed right in the face of the searcher. Ads were carefully placed in the margins, and they weren't called ads; they were called "sponsored links."

Over the next few years, it became clear that this advertising model could be the engine of growth. Google seemed to have learned lessons from the network television industry, which never charged for its programs but made revenue through advertising. The innovative ability to rank the popularity of web pages is one of the core reasons that Google has been able to gain such competitive advantage in its advertising model. Customers purchasing ads are able to see which websites are most frequented and can base their decisions about where to place an ad on that information. In a sense, Google built the equivalent of television-like program ratings for web pages. Likewise, Google found that it could also adopt the television networks' practice of sharing revenue with affiliates in local markets. Google created a successful affiliate model through software such as AdWords that helped product companies advertise on Google and track sales that came from those specific ads.

With the model firmly in place, Google continued to offer new software capabilities to the consumer without charge. These were not simply utilities that were offered to any user. They included electronic mail, shared calendars, and an online word processor and spreadsheet. Although the technology was well designed, the company used clever marketing to create momentum behind its offerings. For example, rather than announcing a new product and working hard to convince customers to try it, Google initiated a program of invitations. Users were "invited" to try out new software.

Each user was given a set of "invitations" that they could use to invite their friends to be part of this exclusive group. Google has repeated this approach with several of the products it has brought to market. Creating an aura of exclusivity helped Google set itself apart from the competition. In addition, Google Mail became the home page for all of the other services that Google offered to its users. From the Gmail page, the user could easily access a calendar, share documents with other Gmail users, send instant messages, and basically collaborate without any messy and cumbersome setup. The company also began offering the same services with a higher level of service to corporate customers. Although they did charge for these services, the cost was well below that of any of its competitors. Google also challenged the telecommunications companies by introducing Google Voice, a system that provides consumers with a phone number that they can use as a voice mail system by forwarding phone calls.

Eventually it became clear that, like Netscape, Google was targeting Microsoft's franchise—the Office suite and Windows operating system. As of this writing Microsoft has not been able to successfully attack Google. First, Google's core assets, its office suite and its collaboration tools, are free so Microsoft has not been able to commoditize them. Although Microsoft has dramatically improved its own search engine with the introduction of Bing, it has not yet been able to take over Google's leadership position. Instead, Microsoft has begun its approach to the market by focusing on customers who purchase airline tickets on the Web and has focused on managing web-based transactions. Likewise, although Microsoft has been offering its own free email services for years via Hotmail, it lacks the cache of Google Mail. And because so much Microsoft revenue comes from its Office franchise, Microsoft has had little incentive to build a parallel franchise around Hotmail. However, Microsoft has not given up and continues to evolve its strategy to try to chip away at Google's competitive advantage.

What is remarkable about the Google sneak attack model is that it is not focused on just one product or one family of products. Rather, Google's vision is broad and deep, based on creating a combination of significant technology innovation with a conventional business model. For example, Google built its own operating system, called Android, based on an open-source model. Open source is commercial-grade software that relies on a community of sophisticated developers who fix technical problems in the code for the good of the entire community. Typically, companies that embrace open source do not charge for the products they create from the open source elements. However, they charge customers for support and any value-added commercial features they implement on top of that platform. This is precisely the model that Google has adopted. Again, it does not charge individual developers fees to license its operating system. For example, it has used Android to become a force in the mobile computing market. It has partnered with Verizon and other telecommunications companies to bring to market products that feature this software. But Google isn't just looking for licensing fees from telecommunication companies; it is looking at the mobile device as another distribution channel for its advertising model. Why the focus on advertising rather than license revenue? It is quite simple: more than 90 percent of the company's revenue comes from advertising. However, Google does have ambitions to expand beyond advertising revenue to better balance the revenue split by selling cloud computing services and potentially other software-as-a-service offerings.[15]

With the rapid growth and importance of cloud computing, Google is an active participant in the game. It has created huge data centers to offer cloud services to users. Its services include an engine that allows developers to build complex cloud applications. This provides Google with a potential leadership role in this increasingly important market that will be the next generation of the Internet.

AMAZON.COM'S WALMART-INSPIRED SNEAK ATTACK

Another company that executed a successful sneak attack strategy is Amazon.com. It was not the first company to start a business of selling consumer goods over the Internet; however, few companies have mastered the model and morphed to address new opportunities as effectively as Amazon has. To the casual observer Amazon .com in its infancy looked like just another online seller of books, but the strategy behind the company was much bigger and more ambitious. Amazon.com took a sneak attack approach to establishing itself as a giant not only in the book industry but also in both the consumer and the technology industries.[16] Had Amazon been obvious from the outset about its plan to challenge the entire retail market, it would have encountered early and swift opposition. If competitors had clearly understood Amazon's ambitions, they would have quickly moved to end the threat. Amazon.com was careful to position itself initially as just an online bookseller, though if you read Amazon's vision statement, it is clear that its goal has always been broader than simply selling books. "Our vision is to be earth's most customer centric company; to build a place where people can come to find and discover anything they might want to buy online."[17]

Amazon.com was founded by Jeff Bezos, a computer scientist who had been an executive in financial services companies before realizing that online selling was his passion.[18] In 1994, when Bezos started Amazon.com, it was already largely apparent that the Internet would become a commercial platform.[19] Bezos decided that the book business could be the launching point for his plan to create a new customer experience for making purchases online. Amazon.com wasn't the first online bookstore; there had been dozens of others. However, instead of trying to take on the book industry and become the biggest and best online bookseller, Bezos' business strategy involved patiently going through the steps necessary to create a compelling online presence.[20] The company created a well-designed website with great navigation that made the act of purchasing a book easy. It also created a new distribution model, providing a revenue stream for smaller, specialized booksellers, who began to use Amazon.com as a distribution channel.

Amazon.com used technology to create an unfair advantage over competitors. This was the beginning of the end for brick-and-mortar companies like Barnes & Noble. At first, it was the booksellers who were threatened by Amazon.com; other retailers didn't really pay much attention. But Bezos and his online site were planning their sneak attack. Meanwhile, competitors were copying the idea of an online bookstore. In 1999, the American Booksellers Associates created BookSense.com to allow customers to order books online from independent bookstores, and Barnes & Noble set up a program to allow customers to order books online and pick them up at their local bookstore.

The mid-1990s were a heady time for the technology sector. Companies with almost no revenue—and certainly no profits—were going public. Therefore, it was by no means a surprise when in 1997, three years after the company started, Amazon.com went public. Amazon.com was in a much stronger position than most of the dot-com companies in the market. The company had a strong business plan, a well-respected brand, and a way to actually make money from the use of the Internet. The company went public at $18.00 a share.

But Amazon.com didn't see its competition as the booksellers—big or small. It was focused on a bigger prize—Wal-Mart. Jeff Bezos wanted Amazon.com to become the Wal-Mart of the online world. This ambition was not lost on Wal-Mart itself. In fact, in 1998 Wal-Mart sued Amazon.com for hiring several of its executives. Wal-Mart's management was beginning to see that the threat from this online bookstore could be real and there was good reason for them to be alarmed by the threat. Amazon.com began building relationships with toy sellers and clothes manufacturers. The little bookstore on the Web was becoming the master online retailer.

It was not a smooth and continuous ride. As with any ambitious company, it hit bumps along the way. When the dot-com crash hit in 2001, it appeared that Amazon might be swept away with other failed online retailers like Pets.com, eToys, and Webvan—to name but a few. But Amazon.com did not give in to the panic. Whereas many dot-coms spent vast sums of money on elaborate marketing campaigns, Amazon.com was obsessed with efficiency. Amazon.com had two factors in its favor: it concentrated on managing its book warehouses in the most efficient way possible, and it provided high levels of customer service. By 2003, nine years after writing his business plan, Bezos's company made its first profit. Four years later, the company made a dramatic change by introducing the Kindle, an e-book reader that allows customers to purchase books online and load them directly onto a small digital reading device. In essence, Bezos had combined the three things that he was good at—online retailing, engineering discipline, and leveraging of technology—to differentiate his company.

Many businesses stay with the strategy of focusing on their "core business" in order to sustain their growth. Thus conventional wisdom would have predicted that Amazon would have continued to focus only on online commerce. Many management consultants would have advised this as the way to go—stick with the core business and expand from there. I suspect that was Bezos's plan. However, something interesting happened along the way. Because Amazon.com had to build a huge computing infrastructure to support its expanding online empire, it had to invest huge amounts of money to ensure that its platform would not suffer slowdowns even when the number of customers grew unexpectedly. Amazon .com wanted to make sure that if a new bestseller hit the market, the customer wouldn't become frustrated because the site was slow and go to another online site or to a bookstore. So the company spent the money and time to build a data center that would provide sufficient capacity no matter how busy the site became.

In establishing this enormous resource, it became apparent that the company had overextended itself. It had more capacity than it needed for the foreseeable future. But luck and pragmatism were on the company's side. Amazon.com decided that it could rent out the excess capacity in its data centers to developers that needed temporary computing capability and extra computing storage. Amazon was lucky, because its excess computing capacity became available just at the time when software companies were open to the idea of renting out computing resources. In the beginning, this strategy offset some costs. Software entrepreneurs and software developers discovered that it was simpler to use incremental computing services than to purchase hardware and software. In essence, this approach to leveraging capacity on demand was responsible for the birth of what we now call cloud computing.

At this stage, Amazon.com combined its luck with its smarts. Amazon.com soon realized that this offering could reap greater benefits than simply offsetting costs. It was, in fact, a new business market. Thanks to Amazon.com's well-established brand in the online selling world and its development of the Kindle reader, it was not a huge leap from there into the computing market. But it wasn't simply because Amazon.com had a good brand and a good reputation that the company thrived. Amazon.com was successful with cloud computing because it fit into the company's core competency—selling low-margin products at a high volume. As with books and consumer goods, when Amazon.com moved into cloud computing it leveraged not just its online site but also a complex ecosystem of partners. The company did not try to offer all computing services itself. For example, to manage its web services platform, it partnered with a myriad of software companies that had this as a core competency. The company wrote software "hooks" that made it easy for these companies to create seamless environments between the Amazon.com services and their own services. This was a wonderful sneak attack strategy. The company did not have to overinvest in developing all of the components to create a robust platform. By partnering with hundreds of eager entrepreneurs, it was able to offer a sophisticated set of capabilities and create goodwill within the technology industry as well as with customers. By opening up the platform, Amazon.com came across not as an aggressor but rather as a benign and helpful partner.

Sneak attacks are a wonderful model for lucky entrepreneurs. The most dangerous stage in an entrepreneur's evolution is when the company begins to gain attention in the market. It is very easy at this stage for a larger and stronger competitor with money and talent to crush an early-stage company. A sneak attack, on the other hand, allows a company to stay under the radar as it builds its long-term strategy.

Lessons Learned

Lesson One: Don't make your ultimate goals obvious. When your company has an innovative product that could challenge market incumbents, you need to be subtle in your approach to the market. Play your cards close to the chest and don't make your long-term strategy obvious to your competitors. Make your company's products and services indispensable to the market before the market incumbents realize that this newcomer is a threat.

Lesson Two: Don't flaunt your initial success. Successful start-ups resist the temptation to equate first success with eventual dominance. Instead, they strive to remain humble. A small company with an unanticipated competitive differentiation needs to execute smartly. Partner with complementary vendors as well as with your competitors.

Lesson Three: Understand your competitors as well as you understand yourself. Too many emerging companies do not

understand the competitive market. To be successful, entrepreneurs need to understand what they are facing. By understanding competitors' motivations and business models, a
company can create a different model that avoids falling
into a trap of complacency, overconfidence, and arrogance.

Lesson Four: Don't let your luck go to your head. Entrepreneurs
are the most optimistic people on the planet. They often look
beyond current reality and envision a future well beyond what
is possible. This can be dangerous for a start-up. Make sure you
are not taking your luck for granted. Transitioning from an
early market requires careful planning and execution. By the
time a market is beginning to mature, well-established companies will be ready to enter the market. To remain competitive, you must get smart and plan well.

As technology markets mature, it is difficult for emerging companies
that have been lucky to transform themselves into leaders. Many
companies that gain recognition in an early market become overly
arrogant and are crushed by better-funded competitors. In a highly
competitive market, a lucky start-up must devise and implement a
well-constructed sneak attack strategy in order to survive.

Luck? I don't know anything about luck. I've never banked on it and I'm afraid of people who do. Luck to me is something else: Hard work—and realizing what is opportunity and what isn't.

—Lucille Ball,
American comedienne

Chapter Five

HERO WORSHIP

Gaining Loyalty by Helping Your Customers Find Personal Success

Successful companies work hard to make their customers successful. If individual employees are able to
leverage the benefits of a technology to get promotions
or new jobs, they will remain loyal. These individuals
become a secret sales team that can help ensure a
company's market success.

Success comes in many shapes and sizes. Some entrepreneurs exploit an innovative technology to address a problem unsolved by existing market leaders. Others find a customer problem and devise the technology to solve that problem. Many mature technology companies look to extend their success by expanding into adjacent markets, often by buying emerging companies. But no matter what path an aspiring entrepreneur or an ambitious CEO takes, success requires a focus on the customer.

The most successful technology companies have always focused on customer pain. When customers find problems with technology or see that existing technology is holding them back from quickly innovating in their business, they look for alternatives. Technology companies tend to position and market their products based on lofty goals of helping customers to innovate and grow. However, in reality individuals buy technology. And individuals have personal reasons why they select one technology rather than another. They may have a strong bond with the sales team, they may believe that one vendor's products are politically the safest choice or, in some cases, employees may believe that if they use a certain product they will have a better chance of getting a promotion or a better-paying job. In other words, employees want to make sure that their skills and their value are important to the companies that pay their salaries. If you target products to the needs of the customer, the decision maker within the customer's organization will be more likely to choose your product, because by choosing your product the decision maker will solve a customer problem and thus receive recognition in the way of promotions, pay raises, or prestige.

Helping individuals achieve success does not mean asking them what they want. There is a big difference between listening to customers and making customers successful. People don't always know precisely what they need at any given time. If you asked a customer five years ago how they would like to use customer relationship management software, how many would have asked that it be implemented on a vendor's server in an unknown site? Probably none. If a company like salesforce.com had asked prospects whether they wanted all their critical customer data in a start-up's data center, it would never have gone into the software-as-a-service business. Salesforce.com based its solution on an understanding of customer pain. The company built on that knowledge and created a solution that customers did not yet know they needed.

POWERSOFT VERSUS GUPTA TECHNOLOGIES

Powersoft and Gupta Technologies are two excellent examples of the do's and don'ts of gaining the loyalty of individual employees within a customer's organization. Both companies had similar technology, but Powersoft focused on building loyalty with individual software developers while Gupta Technologies concentrated on helping customers create elegant and sophisticated software with its software development tools. Both companies were started by entrepreneurs and tackled similar customer problems. Both developed well-designed solutions for their customers. But only one was successful.

Before the Internet became the focal point for the technology industry, a trend called "client/server computing" took the market by storm. The business value of this technology was compelling in the early 1990s. The idea was to use the personal computer as the place where developers would create their software and then link with traditional computing environments such as minicomputers and mainframes to access data and code. The goal of client/server computing was to make computing more accessible to business units, not just the IT department, so that business analysts, marketers, and others could create applications to help answer questions and make business decisions directly from their own PCs, without involving IT.

For the promise of client/server computing to be fulfilled, a new generation of software tools was required to make software development on PCs easy and transparent. This new software development technology had to be capable of working seamlessly with both departmental computers and computers in the data center. This wasn't easy to accomplish in those days. To create programs that made use of the graphical user interface of the PC required that the programmer know exactly where to place images and code on the screen. Only the most experienced and advanced programmers had these skills. This task was certainly beyond the reach of most business analysts. But as with every technology revolution, companies emerged to fill the gap.

In those early days, there were hundreds of companies that emerged to address the problem. Many of them either never got funded or simply couldn't create enough market momentum or raise enough cash to continue, but Powersoft and Gupta Technologies both had enough money and cache in the market to break through and thrive in the early days of the client/server market. Both companies created software that allowed programmers to create PC-based applications that automatically connected to data on servers in the data center or in the business unit, and both focused on the business and IT developers who needed to create software applications that would help make client/server computing a success.

With lots of competition in an emerging market, it can be difficult to have a real impact and gain competitive advantage quickly, whether you are a start-up or an established company. When a start-up business enters a market, it may gain industry attention due to its innovative technology, but lack of adequate funding and name recognition can hold the company back. Customers are often afraid to trust a company without a track record—even when the company offers a potential solution to a problem. In contrast, when an established technology company wants to enter an emerging market, it can be a challenge because their customers are already deeply committed to maintaining the use of existing products. It is not that the customers don't like the new technology; it is just that the company is already spending its time and resources making existing products work. In addition, there is often a steep learning curve for most new technology. When a company is totally focused on servicing its existing customers in a certain way, it can be challenging to see the potential of a new approach that may compete with its current products. The company may experiment with the new technology without changing its old way of thinking and without devoting sufficient resources to win in the marketplace because the business wants to protect the revenue it receives from its current customers who rely on the old product.

How Powersoft Beat the Odds

Powersoft beat the odds. It became the most successful graphical user interface development software company of its era. The company grew very quickly and became very profitable in a short time. After only four years of intense competition and fast-paced growth, Powersoft was purchased by Sybase for almost $1 billion.[1] What made this company so desirable to Sybase?

In 1974 Mitch Kertzman, a veteran entrepreneur, founded Computer Solutions, Inc. (CSI), a custom software development company.[2] By 1981 the company had become a product company with a solution aimed at the needs of small and medium-sized manufacturing companies. The company experienced steady growth over the following fifteen years and gained an installed base of a thousand customers.[3] However, the market was changing by the early 1990s. Customers were asking CSI to add a graphical development environment so that it would be simpler to modify and extend these applications. Unable to find the right commercial products to support customer needs, the company's development team started working on its own solution. It was then that Kertzman was approached by David Litwack, the former head of research and development for Cullinet, a once-successful database company that had been purchased by Computer Associates in 1989. While Litwack was at Cullinet, his team developed a prototype for a graphic development product that Computer Associates wasn't interested in. Litwack felt that this technology could be important if he could get venture capital funding, but that process turned out to be a lot harder than he had anticipated. Kertzman, on the other hand, immediately recognized the value of what Litwack wanted to do, because it addressed the precise problem his company was trying to solve. So rather than raise venture capital, Litwack and his team joined forces with CSI.

What resulted from this collaboration was PowerBuilder, a system that made it easy for programmers to create graphical applications for Microsoft Windows. Before PowerBuilder was introduced, programmers had to write detailed code to tell the system where to place graphical elements on the screen—a tedious and time-consuming process.[4] PowerBuilder was also designed so that a programmer without advanced skills would be able to create sophisticated-looking applications.

The first version of PowerBuilder was released in 1990 with an impressive list of early adopters, including such companies as American Airlines, Microsoft, Fidelity, and 3M. After a short trial period, the full version of the product was released in 1991; within the first six month of the product's release it generated more than $5 million in revenue. By the end of 1992, revenue was up to $22 million and the company was profitable. A year later, the company went public, but by this time, the company's name was no longer Computer Solutions, Inc. The new company name—Powersoft—reflected the success of its new product. Powersoft sold off its manufacturing financial package in order to focus all of its energy on its graphical development system—PowerBuilder.

At first glance, PowerBuilder looked like all of the other platforms being developed to handle graphical software development. Companies ranging from IBM to Oracle to Microsoft, Visix, and Gupta Technologies all provided products aimed at this market. But PowerBuilder captivated the market. Why? As an early consultant to Powersoft, I spent considerable time with both Kertzman and Litwack. What always stayed with me was a conversation I had with Kertzman in those early days. He explained to me that Powersoft was designed specifically to help COBOL developers who were trying to make the transition to graphical development. COBOL (Common Business-Oriented Language), developed in 1959, was one of the original business-focused programming languages and was used by almost every business for decades. In 1997 there were about three hundred billion lines of computer code written; 80 percent of this code was written in COBOL. There were still millions of lines of COBOL code in the market. However, for developers who wanted to have a role in the next generation of software development technology, COBOL was a dead end.

A whole generation of smart COBOL programmers with previously highly prized skills was at risk of becoming obsolete. The typical COBOL programmer had been very successful for decades. Skills in writing COBOL code guaranteed a programmer a good living and a successful career, but as the PC became accepted as a departmental computing platform, companies started to look beyond traditional computing approaches. With the advent of the PC and minicomputer, new languages and new techniques for developing software were emerging. Although COBOL could be used on any platform, other languages were becoming more popular. Therefore, in order to remain relevant, COBOL programmers had to learn new approaches to software development that didn't rely on the traditional centralized computing focus of the previous forty years.

The mainframe computer had been the focal point for computing for decades. However, companies were finding that the mainframe was very expensive, requiring sophisticated and expensive professionals to operate them. At this time in 1980s, the world was changing with the advent of departmental computing driven by the minicomputer and the PC. The emergence of the new client/server computer model allowed the PC to be used as the platform for writing graphical applications that could communicate directly to minicomputers and even the mainframes that were the source of important data. Client/server systems were intended to be used by a business unit rather than the centralized Information Technology department that managed the more complex mainframe environments. Suddenly business units were taking matters into their own hands by writing their own business systems without the oversight of the centralized mainframe IT department.

And there was no chance that business units were about to give up their newfound freedom. Client/server was designed to bring some structure to the chaos of departmental computing. One of the requirements for client/server computing was that the way information appeared on the screen was separate from the database and the programs that developers were writing.[5] However, until this point, no one had figured out how to automate the process of creating PC graphical applications.

Mitch Kertzman and Dave Litwack discovered that they could combine the ease of use of the graphical development with techniques that were well understood by the COBOL programmer. This would allow companies to easily transition COBOL programmers so that they could work in the new environment. It was the best of both worlds—COBOL developers knew the business, which helped the organization, and at the same time they were able to easily update their skills and keep their jobs.

But all platforms were not created equal. Some were designed based on an advanced computer science paradigm called "object orientation." On one level, this advanced concept promised more flexibility and usability to the programmer who could, for the first time, reuse bits of software from one project to the next. Object orientation was one of the most innovative technologies of the 1990s because it promised to revolutionize the way software was built. Rather than rewriting code each time new applications were needed, the developers would be able to reuse the same code over and over again, so they could more quickly assemble the right pieces of code to quickly create new applications.

But the technology was new and unfamiliar and therefore difficult for the typical programmer to learn and use. In contrast, Powersoft decided to focus on creating a system that used many of the principles of object orientation but was designed to be less complex to learn and use based on the skills of the COBOL developer.[6]

Kertzman and Litwack understood their customers very well. After all, Kertzman's company, CSI, had developed software for mid-tier manufacturing companies for decades. These companies needed sophisticated technology, but their employees weren't ready for the state-of-the-art tools. Staff needed technology that was both practical and easy to use. The first priority was to focus on getting business objectives solved quickly and efficiently.

The most valuable customers for their development platform were not the advanced developers. After all, there were only a handful of computer scientists who could deal with that level of complexity. Instead, these entrepreneurs decided that they would concentrate on the COBOL developers. There may have been a few thousand developers hungry to learn the newest pure object-oriented software development techniques, but there were millions of COBOL developers looking for a new lease on life.

Powersoft was focused on certain criteria. First, the development environment had to look good; it had to impress the business unit leaders who wanted something accessible and different. Second, the development environment had to be something that a developer who was used to developing for a traditional mainframe platform could transition to quickly. Therefore PowerBuilder was designed to work in a way similar to a COBOL program—with very clear and concise instructions for how to build an application. While the tool allowed developers to mimic the more sophisticated object-oriented approach to development, the design and deploy approach was similar to COBOL. COBOL developers could take one look at PowerBuilder and understand that this was an environment they could figure out.

The plan worked. When PowerBuilder was announced in 1991, it was quickly adopted by eager customers. Within the first year, the platform became the most popular way for developers to create graphical applications. For the first time, business leaders could look at a computer screen and see a visual image that would help them understand the information stored in their business databases. The former COBOL programmers were suddenly viewed not as overhead but as enablers of change, now that they were the developers creating these applications.

The developers did not take their newfound positions for granted. They understood that their partnership with Powersoft was responsible for their success. Powersoft's marketing was completely focused on the success of this new generation of software developers. They nurtured these new heroes. The company continued to innovate with new capabilities and new ways to help their customers become more valuable to management. Each successful programmer became a salesperson for Powersoft, bringing in new customers through direct marketing campaigns and guerilla marketing campaigns. At that point PowerBuilder's success took on a life of its own. Once the platform reached critical mass, it was no longer viewed as an obscure and unproven technology. It became the incumbent in a new market. Business leaders insisted that it be used within their departments. In fact, Powersoft built its marketing campaigns around how much more personal success a developer would have using PowerBuilder rather than other platforms.

GUPTA TECHNOLOGIES: WHY ELEGANT TECHNOLOGY ISN'T ENOUGH

Powersoft wasn't the only company that sought to reap the benefits of the client/server revolution. Gupta Technologies actually beat Powersoft to market with a graphical development platform. Umang Gupta, a brilliant computer scientist, had worked for both IBM and Oracle Corporation in the 1970s and '80s. But Gupta's real passion was to start a technology company. In 1984, after three years at Oracle, he founded Gupta Technologies. Gupta, like Powersoft, focused on the emerging need for new development technology for client/server. In 1993, when the company went public, it was valued at more than $400 million.[7]

While Powersoft concentrated primarily on graphical development and ease of use, Gutpa and his partner Bruce Scott, also from Oracle, focused on what they knew best—the database. Thus the company produced the first relational database that ran on a PC rather than a large backend system. The product, released in 1988, was called SQLBase. The revenue and growing customer base enabled the company to invest in new technologies. Armed with the PC database, the company took advantage of the emerging requirement for PC-based graphical development and added a new platform. The new product, announced in the early 1990s, was called Team Developer. Like PowerBuilder, Team Developer was focused on making client/server development easier. It included a graphical user interface and an easier way to link the front-end environment to a variety of databases.

Powersoft focused on the COBOL developer; Gupta Technologies was much more concerned with the sophistication of the underlying platform. Gupta was a technology-driven company ahead of its time, and the new environment was based on object orientation, which, again, used sophisticated programming techniques to design software that could be more easily reused in a variety of different situations.[8] There is no doubt that Gupta Technologies created a better-designed set of tools than its competition. While most software relied on 16-bit programming, Gupta made the leap to a more sophisticated and complex 32-bit version.[9] The technology also had capabilities to build a wide range of applications that leveraged client/server technology such as Internet-based development, sophisticated testing, and connecting to a variety of data sources on large backend systems. Why is this important to understand? Gupta was not just far ahead of the market; it was far ahead of the customers it was trying to sell to. In order to make use of the development environment, programmers typically had to know how to write complicated code in addition to using the graphical development tools. Although this could be used to produce a more sophisticated outcome, the typical COBOL developer had a lot of trouble grasping how to work with Gupta's tools. And most of the developers in the market simply didn't have the patience or the knowledge to move to Team Developer. It was too big a transition.

POWERSOFT'S PROBLEMATIC SUCCESS

The client/server market was gaining huge momentum, and Powersoft and Gupta became embroiled in a major battle for the hearts and minds of the client/server developers. While Gupta and Powersoft were the two contenders left standing, ultimately Gupta simply did not have the leverage with the development community that it needed to surpass Powersoft. The COBOL developers, whose fortunes had been transformed by the ease of the transition to PowerBuilder, were fiercely loyal. Powersoft had made the developers its partners, and they became evangelists who brought other developers into the fold.

Unfortunately, Powersoft's enormous success also caused its customers to experience serious performance problems. Although it was easy for the developer to create a graphical application, it was not so easy to maintain that application. Because these applications were easy to create, business management insisted that developers add more and more functionality to projects. Thus the programs became bloated and costly to operate. Powersoft was never able to transition to a more modular model, whereby code could be assembled in a way that was easier to operate and manage. This type of transition would have required the company to create an entirely new software platform. Not only would this have been very costly, but it also would have been very disruptive to the large installed base of customers already using its software.

By 1995, just four years after PowerBuilder was first introduced, this fast-growing segment of the technology market changed again. Powersoft was acquired for almost $1 billion by Sybase, a very big win for the company's shareholders.[10] Gupta's road was rougher. As the company lost ground to Powersoft, a significant part was sold to investors and the name was changed to Centura. Eventually Centura declared bankruptcy and its assets were acquired by Unify, a small company that had been one of the original database development tools popular in the 1980s.[11]

One of the most important lessons we can learn by examining Powersoft and Gupta side-by-side is that it is not always the most sophisticated technology that wins. Entrepreneurs, armed with innovative ideas, often charge into an emerging market, assuming the technology's sophistication will assure success. However, having great technology is only one of the factors that enables a company to win. Being able to make the individual employee successful is equally important, if not more so. Although from afar it may look as though a technology company sells to corporations, in fact the actual buyers are individuals. These individuals want to be recognized in their organizations for making good decisions and achieving good business results. What skills will those individuals gain? Will those skills lead to a better position or more money? Will those individuals be sought after in the market because of the knowledge they have gained? These goals may not sound like the typical technology marketing messages—cost savings to the corporation or improvements of productivity—but although management will make product selection decisions based on their company's business requirements, these decisions are influenced by the decision makers' desire for personal advancement. Therefore technology companies that appeal to the success of the individual decision maker will have a better chance of success than those companies that sell based on technical features alone.

The genius of Mitch Kertzman and Dave Litwack was that they kept their eyes focused on the COBOL programmers who desperately needed a way to preserve their incomes and to remain relevant as technology changed. Had Powersoft simply provided a development environment focused on the new generation of developers, it probably would have failed. Its technology actually had some defects that hurt the company and its customers in the long run. The technology relied heavily on building software to support the PC side of client/server, so the company wasn't able to focus on transferring functionality to backend systems that could have better handled complexity. In essence, it did not allow a balancing of software between the PC and the backend systems. The systems that were developed became cumbersome and difficult to manage. But for a period of time, when there were millions of COBOL programmers who wanted to be heroes again, Powersoft focused on winning their support. The ability to turn individual customers into corporate heroes is a powerful weapon that can change the fortunes of a company that is in the right place with the right technology for the right individuals.

Lessons Learned

Lesson One: Making individuals successful should be a top priority. It is more important to make your customers successful than to have the most sophisticated product in the market. Customers have to be able to get started quickly and find personal as well as business success. Individuals within organizations who are the decision makers or who influence the decision makers are your best ambassadors in the market.

Lesson Two: Continue to innovate even if your product satisfies your customers' needs. Even the most successful company has to understand the weaknesses of their key products. This is very difficult, because technology companies too often become enamored of their own products; these warm feelings are often shared by customers who do not relish change. But without change, technology companies cannot sustain a competitive advantage.

Lesson Three: Be prepared to be your own competitor. Remember what made you successful in the first place. Successful companies fill a market void. So watch for the next market void and establish a separate, unencumbered team that can innovate outside of the internal environment devoted to current products and customers. Look for what will continue to help individuals be heroes in their companies.

It is common for technology companies to focus on creating the most advanced products so as to gain an advantage over the competition. However, the most successful companies focus not only on the technology itself, but, of equal importance, on the individuals within companies who will influence the choice of what technology to buy. Creating heroes is one of the best ways to ensure success.

Luck, that's when preparation and opportunity meet.
—Pierre Trudeau, fifteenth prime minister
of Canada

Chapter Six

LESSONS FROM THE LEMMINGS ERA

How Out-of-Control Dot-Coms
Fueled the Future

When the money flowed like water during the dot-com era, emerging companies developed a range of silly and wonderful technology. Although many of these companies did not survive, they helped influence a new generation of successful ventures that learned important lessons.

The rise and fall of venture-based Internet companies—sometimes referred to as the dot-com era—is an oft-told tale. Traditionally, companies that sought venture capital funding had to demonstrate that they had a significant product offering that was well accepted by early customers and a well-thought-out plan for building revenue in both the short and long term. Venture backers were looking to invest in companies that had already proven their ability to execute and create sustainable companies. The Internet was different from any other computing infrastructure that had been proposed as a standard. First, unlike committees that toiled for years to convince companies to adopt a new approach to standardize communications between systems, the Internet appeared as a fully developed *de facto* communications standard. Developed a decade earlier and widely used by the scientific community, the Internet was the catalyst for change. Therefore the commercialization of the Internet unleashed a revolution in computing. This revolution brought with it a myriad of new companies and technologies, many of which were ahead of their time. Some of these companies were successful, others failed, but much of the technology created during this era was adopted years later by companies that were able to capitalize on the technology at a time when there was an actual need for it.

The dot-com era made a few people very rich—especially the venture capitalists. But many more companies filed for bankruptcy and were never heard from again. It was a time when companies with names like Pets.com, Kozmo.com, Agillion, Amplitude.com, Webvan.com, Intira Corp., govWorks, and countless others that no one remembers became household names. These companies typically raised and lost hundreds of millions of dollars within a few years and then had little or nothing to show for their efforts.

The 2000 Super Bowl illustrates the absurdity of this era. Just as the 1984 Super Bowl was famous for the Orwellian ad that made people pay attention to Apple, the 2000 Super Bowl was famous for the many dot-com company ads it featured. These emerging companies spent millions of their venture capital dollars to promote their underdeveloped products to the world and were essentially pouring that money down the drain. With virtually no revenue and only a few usable products, the party was short-lived. By 2000, the stock market collapsed and these fledgling companies that had spent wildly had no new funding. Most of these companies simply had to close their doors.

I call this period a "lemmings era" because the word "lemming" conjures up the image of a doomed conformist. Lemmings migrate in extraordinarily large groups and many die along the way. During the dot-com revolution a large group of entrepreneurs and investors were caught up in the frenzy of getting rich quickly without any long-range planning. Most of these companies would follow their counterparts lemming-like over the cliff. The investors, entrepreneurs, and customers who were embracing the latest technology trends were doing so without scrutinizing the practicality of those trends.

At least two characteristics epitomize this era: a lemming mentality and an incredible level of innovation. Like a pack of lemmings, entrepreneurs with ideas rushed blindly ahead into the Internet market, but many of them had no plan for how they would turn their new idea into a sustainable revenue model. They were encouraged by countless investors and venture capitalists who rushed to fund any company that was developing an Internet-based product. Few investors at the time examined the business assumptions of the dot-com companies, and few leaders of these companies had a clear business model in mind. Because of this frenzy, there was a lack of discipline in the business plans and strategies of these companies. Logic about what it means to build customer value and create sustainability vanished. These companies raised enormous amounts of money and spent it without a plan. At the same time, the era unleashed a tremendous amount of innovation and creative thinking. Ironically, because these dot-com companies were not constrained to execute on a preordained strategy, their leaders were free to experiment with untested business models and technologies.

Although the vast majority of these companies did not survive the dot-com era, the entrepreneurs that went on to have more successful endeavors learned important lessons they were able to apply in the future. Therefore it is important to understand the dot-com era as a renaissance, in which a few entrepreneurs got rich and others made fortunes selling related products and services such as hardware, space in data centers, marketing services, floor space, and furniture. At the same time, the dot-com era also created lots of interesting ideas and innovations that simply weren't ready for the commercial market. Today these same innovations are common-place with companies like Google, Facebook, Twitter, and sales-force.com. The foundation for the increasingly important cloud computing concept had its origins in the dot-com era. Many of the ideas put forward by the dot-com companies were unsustainable because the technical infrastructure needed to support them did not exist. In addition, the venture capitalists funding the dot-com companies required that they spend the funding quickly in order to go public or simply be acquired. The venture capitalists who funded these companies were more interested in riding the wave of excitement and bringing these start-ups public than in building sustainable companies.

The story of the dot-com era is a tale of incredible promise and innovation; it is also a tale of greed and misdirection. But there are important lessons to be learned, not just about the power of the Internet, but also about how some of these companies were lucky enough to accumulate millions in capital. Those stories of success sent thousands of eager entrepreneurs into the market, many assuming that if they could build a solution, somehow the future would take care of itself. The smart ones were those who both sought out the free-flowing money and constructed a well-thought-out business strategy. But few of the dot-com entrepreneurs planned for the future. Many of these pioneers had innovative ideas that were simply too early to gain wide customer acceptance. Other lucky entrepreneurs who arrived on the scene ten years later with the same ideas became very successful and very wealthy.

The dot-com era began in the mid-1990s because the market was ripe for change. The late 1980s and early 1990s started a revolution in technology unlike anything the world had ever seen. Innovators were searching for a way to transform computing so it could become more like a utility than a series of disconnected systems. Without Internet technology, foundation companies wanting to gain control of a market had to invest hundreds of millions of dollars to build a complex platform and then market that platform to a huge ecosystem of partners and customers. It was not an easy undertaking.

At the dawn of the dot-com era, companies with no business plan, no technology, and certainly no products were flooding the market. At this time I was a computer industry analyst, consulting with both established and emerging software companies about the changing computing landscape. It was common in my role as an industry analyst to have regular meetings with emerging companies to understand how they proposed to bring value to customers. This took place every day. Tech companies would communicate regularly with industry analysts and business reporters in the hope that they would write articles or reports about the company's products. A positive review from an influential analyst could transform the fortunes of a company overnight by lending it instant credibility with investors and early adopters. With enough attention, the company could gain huge traction in the market. In these meetings the executives would describe their technology innovation and how their products would solve critical customer problems. If I liked a particular technology, I might be called upon to talk to a journalist about the product. I might even write a report and mention the product as part of an industry trend.

But something happened in the mid-1990s as the dot-com era began to unfold. I started having meetings with dot-com start-ups. Sometimes I knew these entrepreneurs from other ventures; other times, they seemingly came out of nowhere with their first round of funding, a good portion of which they used to hire prominent public relations firms. Soon I began to notice a pattern. Companies were setting up briefings without a product—and sometimes without an idea! I had to ask what I assumed was an embarrassing question: do you have a product? Astonishingly, many times the entrepreneurs would admit they had no product, just a "wild" idea that they wanted to test out. Many of these entrepreneurs were convinced that if they created a product and offered it to customers at almost no cost, they could then build a substantial customer base to leverage for the future.

This idea, affectionately called "capturing eyeballs," wasn't so far-fetched. But the problem was that even when these entrepreneurs managed to develop a product and offer it to customers, it was unclear whether or not the users were simply experimenting with a free service or if they were serious potential customers who would actually be willing to pay for this service in the future. Most of these entrepreneurs were unable to figure out how to turn these users into paying customers; instead, they focused on the dream of going public and getting rich. Sometimes a company would have a business plan or a specification for a proposed new product. But more often the only plan seemed to be to hit it big and go public.

Why would these CEOs make the rounds of the IT industry analysts and members of the press? They were seeking publicity as well as reactions and advice. So analysts like myself were the equivalent of a focus group or some sort of Rorschach test. Occasionally the ideas were actually well thought out; other times they were crazy ideas that never would—and never *should*—see the light of day. Sometimes there would be a germ of an idea. For example, I remember a company planning a business to offer digital picture frames that would be connected to the Web. Clearly this was a good idea. Some fifteen years later, retailers like Walmart and Target made this work; but these behemoths were far different from the small start-up of the dot-com era, armed with a few million venture capital dollars and no sustainable strategy. There were companies that provided customer relationship management software as a service well before salesforce.com or NetSuite were formed. There were Internet service providers like Exodus Communications that provided cloud computing services a decade before that market emerged. Although conventional wisdom would have you believe that all the technology from the dot-com era was based on silly ideas, there were many great ideas that required an infrastructure, such as pervasive consumer broadband access, that did not yet exist. Many of these ideas laid the groundwork for some of the most successful companies in the market today.

AGILLION: THE PRECURSOR TO SOFTWARE AS A SERVICE

Imagine a service that enabled customers to sign up for a sales management system on the web, paying a monthly fee per user. Imagine that that service also was focused on small and medium-sized businesses and incorporated a way for business partners, such as credit card companies, to offer their services. This sort of technology is widely used today, but in 1998 it was revolutionary. The story of Agillion is an example of a company with the right idea at the wrong time. Smart but not lucky. The market just wasn't ready.

In 1998, two veterans of the computer industry, Steve Papermaster and Frank Moss, got together and raised $40 million from Goldman Sachs, Cisco, and Morgan Stanley.[1] Papermaster had started a successful software and consulting firm called BSG Systems in 1987. Moss was the CEO of Tivoli (later sold to IBM for almost $800 million) from 1991 to 1997 (later, he served as the director of MIT's Media Lab from 2006 to 2010). Their plan was bold and ambitious. Their new company, which they called Agillion, was an application service provider designed as a marketplace for small businesses to buy and sell services. Agillion's technology was designed to allow these companies to create a customized web page for each of their clients.[2] As part of its initial go-to-market plan, Agillion was hoping to offer access to the commerce platform to customers for a very low price and deploy an advertising/sponsorship model to large retailers such as Office Depot.[3] Agillion also planned to use an extensive partner channel to deliver the service to small and midsize businesses. But the company spent its money too quickly—even buying a spot during the Super Bowl. More important, the supporting infrastructure wasn't mature enough to support widespread adoption of the platform. By 2001, unable to raise a second round of funding, the company declared bankruptcy.[4]

Although Agillion ultimately failed, the idea itself was excellent. In fact, it is the same idea behind salesforce.com—one of the most successful software-as-a-service companies today. But it was Agillion that first came up with this strategy and the company that was formally launched in 1998—a year before salesforce.com opened its doors.[5]

BROADBAND SPORTS: A PREMATURE ATTEMPT AT ONLINE SPORTS

When one thinks about the companies that have successfully aggregated sports online, the first name that comes to mind is ESPN, owned by Disney. ESPN has managed to corner the market in online sports both nationally and within local markets. And they aren't the only power. Yahoo! Sports has a successful model, as does FoxSports.com. But before any of these powerhouses emerged, there was Broadband Sports.

Broadband Sports was created in 1998 with over $60 million in funding from Michael Dell, Dell Computer's founder; Frank Biondi Jr., former executive of Universal Studios, Inc.; Redpoint Ventures; and Sequoia Capital.[6] The company's goal was to become a go-to site for sports content over the Web. In the company's SEC Forms S-1 filing for its public offering in November 1999, it stated that its mission was to be "a leading Internet provider of original content and commerce for hundreds of individual sports communities. These geographically dispersed communities are composed of fans who follow individual sports, teams and athletes and are characterized by a passionate demand for content and commerce relating to their particular interests."[7] The company had an aggressive marketing plan and signed agreements with major sports figures, and it entered into partnerships with companies like AOL, eBay, Fox, ESPN, and Yahoo.[8]

Clearly Broadband Sports had a great idea. The company even raised an additional $20 million in 2000. However, at the time, the company was breaking new ground. It was lucky enough to be in the right place at the right time, but if it was to be sustainable it had to combine that luck with the right management strategy. The model of aggregating sports content was new. The company's partners, such as ESPN and Yahoo, were still evolving their own online strategies. They weren't convinced that they should cede control of a potentially multi-billion-dollar market to an upstart. In retrospect, it appears that Broadband Sports' innovative strategy was premature. The company simply did not have the market power to fight against much bigger players that already had well-established strategies with sports franchises. The company's ideas and innovations, however, arc commonplace today. Unfortunately for Broadband Sports, its timing was off, and it could not withstand both the dot-com crash that cut off the money supply and the competitive threats. Broadband Sports understood the technology it would need to build an online sports franchise, but it lacked the business commitment to tackle such a competitive market. By early 2001, the company shut down.[9]

EXCITE@HOME: COMBINING CABLE AND INTERNET BEFORE THE MARKET WAS READY

It is common today to purchase Internet, cable, and telephone services from a single provider. Companies like Cabletron, Time-Warner, AT&T, Comcast, and Verizon are competing with each other in exactly this market. But before these companies came out with their offerings, there was a dot-com company that pioneered the concept. Excite@Home introduced many innovations in terms of both the technology and the business model that no one had seen before.[10] But the market was too immature, and customers were not ready to buy. Partners were confused about the potential for revenue.

@Home, a provider of high-speed Internet services, was born in the mid-1990s, just as the Internet boom was gaining momentum. One of the catalysts for this momentum was the Telecommunications Act of 1996 (the first overhaul of U.S. telecommunications laws in sixty-two years). This legislation enabled cable companies to offer Internet-based services for the first time. The act spurred a flurry of activity, which included the partnering of an entrepreneur named Milo Medin with three cable providers—TCI, Comcast, and Cox Communications—to create a company called @Home and establish high-speed Internet services. At one point, @Home had more than four million subscribers. The company went public in 1997 and, through this offering, raised almost $95 million. Theoretically this should have been a successful venture: Internet services were exploding, and cable companies, with their infrastructure and installed base, should have been well positioned to exploit this demand. But in reality, cable companies simply weren't ready for the new business model. They understood television, but not the Internet. There was an immediate clash of cultures between the Internet entrepreneurial culture and the cable business culture. By the end of 1997, the company had lost more than $22 million. It was clear that the business model wasn't working. To change the dynamics of the business, @Home decided to acquire Excite.

Excite was a web search engine founded by six Stanford University students in 1993.[11] It went public in 1996 with less than $15 million in revenues and no profits. Despite the fact that it sold shares to fund the purchase of other companies in an effort to gain a leadership position in the market, and despite a myriad of significant partnerships, Excite was able to generate only $154 million in revenue by the end of 1998, the last quarter that the company showed positive cash flow. It did not know how to use its cash while integrating its acquisitions, so it floundered. What was appealing about Excite was that it had created a big persona and established both a brand and a customer base. @Home purchased Excite for $6.7 billion in the biggest merger of two Internet companies up to that time. The newly minted company, Excite@Home, was to be a full-service Internet provider, including high-speed Internet services with a search engine and content portal.[12]

But alas, the new business model was no more effective than before the merger. The merged companies continued to seek acquisitions to try to boost their offerings, buying a company called iMail to manage customer orders and payments, an online greeting card company called BlueMountain.com, and even a photo-sharing company called Webshots. But the company had no overall business strategy, no vision for the future, and no roadmap for how these acquisitions fit into a comprehensive plan for long-term sustainability. Ironically, the only segment of the company that was making money was its basic Internet service. Advertising revenue declined. By the fourth quarter of 2000, the company's stock value had dropped by 90 percent. And the news only got worse. In an effort to stay in business, the Excite@Home entity had borrowed too much money. It began to try to restructure the company and sell assets. But nothing seemed to help. Finally, in October 2001, the company filed for Chapter 11 bankruptcy protection. The company's most valuable asset, its high-speed network, was sold to AT&T.

As was the case with many other dot-com ventures, Excite@Home had plenty of good ideas that would eventually become business models for companies like Google, Microsoft, Yahoo, and Comcast. Excite@Home had been smart enough to pick the right approach—the Internet as the infrastructure for computing and search, combined with advertising and content to drive revenue.[13] However, the company's downfall was its arrogance, its lack of sufficient attention to the original business model, and its ineffective utilization of substantial cash. In the end, the company simply ran out of time and money. With smarter planning and better cash management, the company might have succeeded. But it certainly provided important lessons for the next generation of Internet companies.[14]

During the dot-com era, thousands of companies had experiences similar to those discussed in this chapter. Many of these companies were lucky enough to be at the right place as the Internet emerged as the foundation for computing for the next millennium. These entrepreneurs were smart enough to understand the huge potential of the Internet to create enormously successful companies. But it could be argued that the very conditions that made the era so extraordinarily successful for a few were responsible for many of the failures that it witnessed. Money was just too easy to get. An entrepreneur simply had to have a rudimentary business plan, based on a single idea—some brilliant, others ludicrous. The venture backers were also taken in by the sometimes irrational exuberance of the decade and never asked the hard questions. Thus few of these lucky entrepreneurs and investors had the foresight to plan for the future. Many of the most insightful executives were simply too early in the evolution of the Internet market to achieve their dreams.

Lessons Learned

Lesson One: Create a long-term and well-thought-out strategy. Entrepreneurs in the dot-com era were lucky enough to live in a climate that enabled them to raise vast sums of money. Although money helps, it is not a substitute for a long-term and well-planned strategy. That strategy must be based on creating technology that cannot be easily duplicated by more established competitors. During a lemmings era there are lots of venture capitalists looking to cash in on an emerging market. Therefore, although it is worthwhile to leverage the market momentum of a lemmings market, you need to create a strategy that anticipates predictable customer needs and delivers on that promise.

Lesson Two: Create a plan that allows for emerging technology to mature. The most pragmatic strategy is to combine an emerging technology with a more mature offering. It is sometimes better to experiment and prepare for the forthcoming technology without overcommitting too early. Combining a mature technology with an emerging one will allow you to hedge your bets.

Lesson Three: Do not assume that market leaders will support your strategy. During the dot-com era, emerging companies came up with innovative ideas that assumed they would be lucky enough to upend market leaders. Many dot-com companies were smart enough to design very creative strategies that could revolutionize everything from how television was delivered to how consumers would buy products and content. However, they were not smart enough to realize that market leaders would never give up their power to an ambitious upstart. Make sure that your strategy includes a competitive technology advantage that doesn't rely on the benevolence of bigger and more powerful competitors.

Lesson Four: Pay attention to patterns of failure. During the dot-com era it was easy to focus on overly optimistic projections of market growth and readiness. Few start-ups paid attention to the reasons that companies were failing, so they wound up repeating the same mistakes. Applying lessons to new market segments can prepare entrepreneurs for future success.

Lesson Five: Pay attention to customer problems. Few entrepreneurs in this emerging market paid enough attention to solving customer problems. As a result, they were either too far ahead of the needs of the market or unable to offer a product that customers were ready for.

The dot-com era spawned a huge number of companies with many innovative ideas. Agillion was a pioneer in the field of offering software as a service. Broadband Sports had the innovative idea of providing a destination site for sports content online. Excite@Home understood the potential of bringing together Internet, cable, and telephone as a common platform to serve a community of buyers. These companies—and many like them—had the potential to turn their markets upside down. But all had a common fatal flaw: they failed to fully understand the dynamics of the markets they were trying to capture. The dot-com companies weren't just building technology companies. They had the unbridled ambition to think that they could transform established markets through innovative technologies. Many were smart enough to see what was possible by applying the Internet to commerce in ways never envisioned. However, they were also arrogant and assumed that the money they had raised would be enough to ensure success.

Their grand experiments did accelerate change. Moreover, they taught important lessons to future entrepreneurs about planning, creating competitive differentiation, and preparing for the long term.

*If a man who cannot count finds a four-leaf clover,
is he lucky?*

—Stanislaw J. Lec, poet and aphorist

Chapter Seven

THE GOTCHA SYNDROME
Why Promising Technologies Fail

The gotcha syndrome happens when a technology trend that promises to deliver a complete solution unpredictably falls short, leaving more than a few devastated entrepreneurs in its wake. When customers grapple with complicated business situations, they seek out emerging technologies as a potential way to deal with problems. Many emerging technologies—such as artificial intelligence, object orientation, open systems, and client/server computing—promised to unlock the secret to success. However, all of them had unforeseen problems and unanticipated outgrowths—the gotcha syndrome.

Whether you're talking about innovations in software or any other industry, there are always tantalizing developments that promise to solve intractable problems. But typically the first generation of an emerging technology doesn't get it right. Sometimes the new technology simply doesn't work. Other times the approach to solving the problem is right, but the implementation is off target. I call this the "gotcha syndrome"—an innovation that holds out great promise but, because of unforeseen or unexpected problems, fails to fulfill its promise. Ironically, most gotchas in technology are innovations that require more maturation before success is achieved, so it is important not to dismiss them. The fundamental knowledge from these experiments can provide a solid foundation for future success.

Typically, new technologies are introduced with lots of fanfare. Venture capitalists are always looking to place their bets on winners. The term "first mover advantage" becomes the mantra, as companies vie for dominance in new markets. The theory goes, if you can be the first company to create a product that addresses an emerging market, you will win. Occasionally some financial backers and entrepreneurs get very rich commercializing an emerging technology early in its evolution. Usually, however, success comes more slowly, if at all.

Sometimes a new idea captures the imagination of the market and gains huge traction, but little revenue. Such ideas have merit because they have the potential to solve critical business problems. Therefore customers are often willing to experiment with these technologies to see if, in fact, they can deliver on their promise. Artificial intelligence and object orientation are two such ideas. They are both extremely important technologies that have become the underpinnings of many important products. In their early days, both of these technologies appeared to have huge potential as standalone markets. Enormous sums of money were poured into products attempting to exploit these markets, but then, within a few years, the commercial market for these technologies evaporated, and most of the companies that invested in them went out of business.

Artificial Intelligence: Not Commercially Viable

Research into artificial intelligence began in earnest in the 1950s; by the early 1980s commercial companies were exploring the possibility of using AI-based programming techniques to create a commercial market. The first commercial product, an expert system, was designed by Carnegie Mellon University for Digital Equipment Corporation. DEC discovered that by implementing business rules into software to automate routine and repetitive tasks, it could save significant expenses. This could be done by translating business judgment into these programs. The experiment caught the attention of many companies who saw the potential of repeating DEC's success. An industry focused on helping companies save huge amounts of money was born.

But long before this commercial market began to take shape, in 1955 John McCarthy, an American computer scientist, had coined the term "artificial intelligence." He defined it as "the science and engineering of making intelligent machines."[1] The first glimmer of potential for a commercial application in the artificial intelligence market began in the 1970s: it promised that robots could be programmed to do tasks, freeing up time for people both at home and in the workplace. The problem with artificial intelligence was the amount of effort that a customer had to invest to input information about its business practices before it could use the system in a practical way. Also, the base technology was priced out of the reach of all but the most cash rich companies. Investing millions of dollars for an unproven technology was too risky for most companies. Ironically, companies that developed products using artificial intelligence, though not successful themselves, laid the groundwork for many successful products. Artificial intelligence is now embedded in countless innovations across a vast number of industries.[2] It is the foundation for robotics used for surgery and for emergency repairs in deep water. It underpins the ability of search engines to determine the context of questions, and it is used to help determine when a system's component is about to fail.

OBJECT ORIENTATION: UNMANAGEABLE AND UNPREDICTABLE

Object-oriented programming first appeared in the 1960s as an answer to the complexity of writing business applications. Xerox PARC (Palo Alto Research Center), the innovative research laboratory, developed the first object-oriented programming language called Smalltalk in the early 1970s. Object-oriented programming is a technique for creating software elements that are self-contained. An object executes one specific task—drawing a line, calculating an average, or making a ball spin on a screen. Because each element is independent, it can be combined with other elements to create complicated programs.[3] The promise of object orientation was huge. A developer could create one piece of code that could be used over and over again. For example, if every element used in creating an application could be reused, programming could be reduced to an assembly process. The unanticipated problem—the gotcha—of object orientation was that each developer had his or her own technique for creating code that was intended to be shared. Enthusiastic programmers would write hundreds and perhaps thousands of small programs to be reused by others. However, there was no easy way to identify what that piece of code should be used for or even where it was stored. Was the piece of code well constructed and trustworthy? Would it deliver on its promise? No one knew and, as a result, the early experiments with object orientation failed to create a viable market. But, like artificial intelligence, object-oriented technology held great promise; today it is the foundation for modern computer languages, service-oriented architectures, cloud computing, and social networks.

OPEN SYSTEMS: AN APPROACH, NOT A MARKET

Another technology trend in the gotcha syndrome category was the open systems movement.[4] An open system was a common software platform that was not owned and controlled by a single vendor. In the mid-1980s large companies dominated significant markets and charging high prices. IBM dominated with the mainframe computer; Digital Equipment Corporation and Wang Laboratories, with the minicomputer. Open systems would make it possible for smaller vendors with fewer resources to compete. If a start-up could use sophisticated and freely available technology that they didn't have to pay licensing fees to use and did not have to develop themselves, they could compete with much larger companies that spent huge amounts of time and money to develop technology. Like artificial intelligence and object-oriented technology, open systems technology had great potential, but again there were unforeseen problems. The open systems software was an enabler, not a differentiator. Therefore, although customers might be pleased that their vendors were not using a proprietary environment that would lock them in, these customers wanted to see solutions that solved their problems.

In the late 1980s and early 1990s hundreds of companies were creating software that was not tied to a single hardware platform. They differentiated themselves based on their use of an operating system called Unix. The operating system was designed in 1969 for use in AT&T's phone network. However, because of an antitrust settlement signed in 1956, AT&T was prohibited from entering the computer industry and couldn't commercialize its operating system. To adhere to the terms of the consent decree, AT&T was required to license the operating system to any nontelephone company. Because of this, not only was it licensed by commercial computer companies, but universities and start-ups also found it to be a practical approach to gaining access to leading-edge technology at little or no cost. This accidentally spawned the practice of community involvement in the development of sophisticated software. The unexpected upshot of the open systems movement was that it turned out to be not a market at all, but rather a catalyst that, a decade later, helped many of the Internet companies bring compelling products to market in record time. Open systems was, in reality, a philosophy and an approach to beginning to solve customers problems. It never became an actual market. Companies that tried to sell their technology based only on the fact that they were open had a difficult time solving customer pain.

Today, open systems, in the form of open-source software, have dramatically helped hundreds of important companies like Amazon .com, Facebook, and Google. All use open-source technology, including the follow-on to Unix, called Linux. Although Unix became an open-source offering by decree, Linux became an open-source operating system by design. One of the characteristics of open systems is that no one company controls the evolution of the software—whether it is an application, an operating system, or a computer language. With a community process, these volunteers, some of which are commercial companies, contribute their ideas and code, combined with fixes to broken code, for the good of the overall market. The sophistication of this approach has led to an incredible amount of innovation. Entrepreneurs with great ideas could start companies with little or no capital, because they did not have to invest in developing the underlying software elements—they could leverage the freely available open-source software. Had there not been a huge growth and acceptance of open systems and open source, the market for technology-based products might have evolved in a completely different way. There certainly would not have been the kind of innovation that came out of universities and start-ups across the globe.

THE CLIENT/SERVER MARKET: LACK OF INFRASTRUCTURE

There are many important lessons to be learned from technology innovations that had a few years of spectacular growth and then fizzled—only to be reborn as successful products in a new generation. Because the Internet is now so globally pervasive and commonplace, it is easy to forget that this wasn't always the case. But it is important to recognize that, before the Internet emerged as a foundation of computing, there was another technology that set the stage for the emergence of the Internet but suffered a gotcha syndrome fate—namely, client/server technology. The client/server market fell victim to the gotcha syndrome because it lacked a common supporting infrastructure that customers could rely on. Each vendor had to start from scratch and build a proprietary platform, which was difficult for vendors to build and even harder for customers to manage. Like other gotcha syndrome victims discussed previously—artificial intelligence, object orientation technology, and the open systems movement—client/server computing offered immense potential and, although imperfect, set the stage for future successful enterprises.

Client/server computing was one of the most important technology trends of the 1990s. It was the first stage in the radical transformation of enterprise computing from a tightly controlled and centralized resource to a highly distributed Internet-based model. With the advent of client/server, computing started to become the engine of innovation at the departmental level. However, the client/server market began to fail as its ability to keep up with customer demand was unsustainable. Because no one had tried to create this type of flexible approach to distributing computing without a centralized mainframe, there was no roadmap for pioneers to follow. The resulting client/server systems were too unpredictable and difficult to manage.

Client/server technology was intended to help business users create systems more easily than was possible with the much more complex mainframe systems. In solving that problem, client/server created new problems. First, in the client/server model the PC was the computing environment where application code was developed and then deployed for users to access their information by communicating messages between the PC and the "servers" or systems. However, PCs had not been designed to serve this function, so they were difficult to manage as the way to design software. Second, client/server made the assumption that the PC could efficiently and quickly communicate with the server and that information could easily be sent and received between the two. Communications technology simply wasn't good enough to support the type of data exchange needed to meet customer expectations. Customers expected to be able to create extremely sophisticated software very quickly with the same performance that they had achieved with mainframe systems. However, the technology wasn't sophisticated enough to handle this level of complexity. Because of the immaturity of existing technologies, each vendor had to invest in an entire computing software platform to support the interaction between software elements. Client/server vendors were able to gain some early success because of pent-up customer demand. However, it would be another five years before the Internet emerged as a pragmatic and standardized underlying platform to support a new generation of computing.

Obviously, software technology does not appear on the market fully developed. There is much trial and error before a technology evolves to become mainstream. If a company has initial success with an innovative emerging technology that has begun generating revenue, it is difficult for the company to suddenly change direction. It is common for managers to become so enamored of their own strategy and technology that they lose perspective and fail to anticipate market change; this happened to many people who had invested in the client/server market. Unfortunately, the "gotcha" here is that the technology needed an infrastructure that simply wasn't available at the time; hence, as the Internet emerged as a better alternative infrastructure for computing, the client/server market collapsed. Some vendors saw the changes coming and reacted; others simply watched from the sidelines as their revenue declined and customers left to adopt more flexible technology options.

Client/server computing was among the most complex technology architectures to emerge after the mainframe. In many ways, the client/server leaders were trying to reconstruct the capabilities and functions of the mainframe within the bounds of a more flexible model. During the client/server era, the smart entrepreneurs focused so much on creating complex, sophisticated software that they lost track of the customers' need for simplicity. The companies that did the best in terms of revenue growth were those that came out with less-sophisticated software that was easier for customers to use. Their solutions might not have been as sophisticated as those of their "smarter" counterparts, but they had an easier time attaining market sustainability.

Why Client/Server Failed

There are some important lessons to be learned from the rise and fall of client/server computing. Like many other technology innovations that become major industry forces, client/server computing started as a potential solution to customer problems. Until the 1980s, when the PC suddenly became a phenomenon with business users, computing was tightly controlled. It was such an expensive resource that the idea of decentralized computing didn't make sense. As PCs and minicomputers arrived on the scene, it was suddenly possible to rethink the economics of computing. But the early days of distributed or decentralized computing were awkward. PCs were relegated to disconnected functions such as word processing and spreadsheets; minicomputers were used for departmental applications that were isolated from the centralized computing of the corporate IT department. Communications technologies were so immature that, although a file could potentially be moved from one system to another, real connectivity and interoperability between departmental systems with centralized IT was slow and unpredictable. As PCs and minicomputers became mainstream, it was becoming clear that supporting these incompatible and disconnected silos of technology was impacting a company's ability to manage its technology assets.

The client/server era took shape because of immediate problems that needed to be solved. If computing technology was to be the engine of business growth there was a need to make software development much easier. As I discussed in Chapter Five, it was difficult to place images on a computer screen so as to allow a businessperson to work with a system because software developers had to write code to place those images on the screen. This was cumbersome and complicated and even the most sophisticated software looked quite crude on the computer screen. As minicomputers and PCs became standard in most corporations, the industry needed a way to make those systems more accessible to the business. This would require a revolution in software development that didn't require the programmer to anticipate precisely how the characters and images would appear on the screen. This movement toward a more graphical development environment was the most important and most lasting innovation of the client/server era. It offered the opportunity for a less-sophisticated developer who was not an engineer or computer scientist to create an application that was easier to program and use. Even more important, it allowed those applications to be changed rapidly as business needs changed. Today this is the customary way software is designed.

The early success of any emerging technology always leads to unanticipated consequences. Typically, these unanticipated consequences sow the seeds of failure because, as emerging technologies gain traction in business markets, innovative developers tend to push the technology beyond its intended use. These failures often signal the beginning of the end for lucky companies that were in the right place at the right time. On the other hand, they also present new opportunities for product innovation.

One of the biggest drawbacks of client/server computing is something I call the "fat client syndrome." Client/server's graphical development approach made it very easy for unsophisticated developers to build applications, in contrast to the complex process of building mainframe applications. But the resulting applications were often too big and too poorly designed, and therefore harder to manage. In a previous generation of technology, a business executive would look at a computer screen and have no idea how an application worked. He simply had to trust that the IT organization was executing on their requirements—whether or not IT was capable of doing so. Certainly there was plenty of frustration because of the time, effort, and money required to create software. With the sudden development of the graphical user interface and the graphical development environment, the business user could see the hidden potential of technology. For the first time, the executive could actually see what the software was doing. The screen showed how data was being manipulated, and business managers could describe precisely what they wanted to see. These results could be completed in a fraction of the time and with a fraction of the effort required by the older generations of technology.

In the early days of client/server computing, business managers were satisfied with the results they were seeing. Business leaders were able to visualize their data and their business needs as never before. But, as typically happens with these "gotcha" technologies, the devil is always in the details. "Gotcha" technology usually seems to achieve results more quickly and easily than anything anyone had ever seen before. It seems too good to be true—and it typically is. This is particularly so when an innovation solves a problem created by a previous generation of technology and at the same time creates new problems. So it was with the first generation of client/server. Many of the development systems were designed to perform routine tasks. However, there was so much pent-up demand from business users that they insisted on pushing the technology beyond its intended use. Expectations exploded. Business customers wanted more and more functionality, assuming that it would be as easy to achieve as the initial capabilities. As often happens with first-generation innovation, the developers of the technology had to find ways to meet the needs of an ever-more-demanding customer base. Competition increased as more venture capitalists wanted to fund companies in this potentially transformative and lucrative market.

To meet business requirements, customers found ways around the limitations of client/server technologies. Vendors had to supplement the graphical tools with low-level, complicated programming tools. Therefore the promise of easy graphical software development with no programming proved to be an illusion. No longer could these vendors guarantee that this new technology was completely different from the old solutions. And there were unanticipated complexities. Projects became too complicated, and developers who had an easy time in the early days now were having trouble satisfying customers. Vendors had also promised customers that the client/server environment would be much less expensive to build and operate than mainframe computing. However, project and management costs of these client/server projects started to increase dramatically. The hope that client/server would make computing much cheaper and more efficient started to fade.

The application initially built with a graphical development tool was fast and inexpensive. However, as time progressed, developers had to add more functions and more capabilities to meet the demands of business. So the fast application now became much slower and more unwieldy, which in turn required businesses to purchase bigger PCs with more memory and more disks. Soon each desktop device was costing as much as $10,000 to $20,000. And if a business wanted to have three hundred analysts use these applications, the PC platform to support client/server environments could cost as much as $6 million, not including the costs of the software and the server that the PCs needed to communicate with. If a business wanted to ensure that there was ubiquitous availability of these applications, costs became astronomical. And that was only the beginning of the problems for the client/server market.

Even when a development team was disciplined enough to create more streamlined applications, these applications were difficult to manage. Each department might create dozens of different client/server applications, but who made sure that these applications adhered to company policy? Who made sure that the data that was streaming into these applications and onto the desktops of business users was correct? The answer: no one had really thought about the consequences of distributing computing systems throughout business units across the company, and it turned out that allowing so many different systems to easily communicate with each other was much more complicated than anyone had imagined. Mainframe computing had solved this problem decades earlier by simply providing a centralized, tightly integrated set of capabilities. Client/server computing had none of the rigor required to ensure that the components worked together as a unified system. There was no software on the market to help companies create a logical design for how the application should actually operate to help the business. What would be the component parts? How would they relate to each other? What were the business policies that should be written into these systems?

There was another problem: once these systems were built, how would the communications between the various systems be managed? There wasn't any type of management capability built into these systems to manage and monitor the performance. The more day-to-day operations came to depend on client/server systems, the more the immaturity of the technology was exposed.

By the mid-1990s, there were hundreds of companies in the client/server business. And at this point, it wasn't simply the early innovators I talked about in Chapter Five, like Powersoft and Gupta Technologies. The larger market leaders, like Microsoft and IBM, had entered the market with major product introductions and massive marketing efforts. Companies like SAP, which focused primarily on huge mainframe packaged applications for capabilities such as accounting, were investing heavily in transforming their products for the client/server architecture. Entrepreneurs were selling their immature companies to large companies that did not want to be left out of this emerging market. It appeared that the market momentum would continue unabated. But customers were starting to have second thoughts, because product implementations were growing too complicated and expensive.

As often happens in emerging markets, vendors heavily invested in the market were not paying attention to increasingly loud customer complaints. Consultants and market analysts began pointing out warnings, but their warnings went unheeded. Instead of recognizing the seriousness of customer discontent, vendors looked for solutions to market contraction by establishing more partnerships, opening more sales offices in more countries, and bringing in new management.

The Second Generation of Client/Server: Too Much Complexity

Clearly, the first-generation tools to create graphical client/server environments were having problems. The market leaders—including Powersoft, Gupta, and Microsoft—were struggling to keep their customers satisfied. They added new functionality to help increase the usability of their products, but it was becoming clear that for customers to be able to use them to solve more complicated business problems, the products would have to change.

Although the focus of the first generation was to solve the complexity of how information was presented to the business user, the second generation tackled the ways in which these environments communicated with other systems and information was integrated across the enterprise computing environment. While early innovators—Powersoft, Gupta, Visix, and hundreds of others—struggled to add enterprise features to their platforms, a new breed of vendors entered the market. The upstarts didn't have the baggage of their predecessors. They also had learned lessons from the pioneers and were able to create products better suited to customer needs.

The two most prominent companies that grabbed the attention of the enterprise client/server market in its second generation were Forte and Dynasty Technologies. Both companies were founded in 1991—around the same time that Powersoft and Gupta were already becoming market leaders. But because Powersoft and Gupta were focused on customers' immediate need for graphical software development, they gained prominence and revenue growth before either Dynasty or Forte was fully developed.

Although Dynasty and Forte addressed the same need for a system to address more complex enterprise software requirements, the two companies could not have been more different. Forte focused on developing a software development and management system that was built from the bottom up to handle the complete technical computing environment. In contrast, Dynasty started from the business process and built a system whereby the customer used a set of predesigned components to customize the computing environment. The developers would then use these rules to generate new software code. The differences in approaches were a direct outgrowth of the background of the founders.

Forte was founded by three technologists with deep roots in the computer industry.[5] Marty Sprinzen, CEO, had been an executive with Ingres, one of the relational database pioneers. Paul Butterworth, the chief technologist, was also a veteran of Ingres. The third partner, Michael Hedger, head of European operations, came from Oracle Corporation. Although their focus in the market was on graphical development, Forte focused its innovation on the ability to separate the functions of software into component parts to make the software easier to manage. But the company didn't stop there; it had a vision of, in essence, duplicating all of the computing capabilities traditionally handled by the mainframe. For example, it developed techniques for managing complex business transactions, developing complex business applications, and providing the communications infrastructure between components. The company was intent on differentiating itself by being independent of any single hardware or operating system platform.

Armed with $30 million in venture funding, the Forte management team had very ambitious plans.[6] In addition to its funding, the company had created huge anticipation in the market even before its product was complete. In fact, at this early stage it was able to establish partnerships with many of the major players, including Apple Computer, Data General, Digital Equipment, and IBM. Some market watchers believed that Forte had the potential to become the next Microsoft. To achieve its ambitions as quickly as possible, the company followed what had become a well-known path—it went public in 1996 with approximately $30 million in sales. Three years later, the company had succeeded in growing to $80 million in revenue (by the end of its last fiscal year before it was acquired)—but without a profit. Had the Internet and web software development been available before Forte designed its software, it would have been in a stronger position to survive. Also, it did not have the benefit of Sun's Java language, which was introduced after Forte had already invested in designing its own development tools. Java was becoming the preferred language for developing the new generation of software. As it became clear that Forte's vision was bigger than its ability to execute, Sun Microsystems purchased Forte for $500 million as part of its expanding portfolio of software offerings.[7]

Like Forte, Dynasty Technologies, had grand ambitions of becoming the leader of the second generation of the client/server market. Dynasty was founded by Michael Lyons, an entrepreneur who had previously started a firm called Catalyst Corporation, a company that focused on reengineering business processes.[8] Catalyst was sold to Peat Marwick, at the time a large accounting/systems integration firm. After spending several years as a partner at Peat Marwick, Lyons struck out on his own again. This time he became president of a company called Asyst Technologies, Inc., which created one of the earliest commercial repository technologies for keeping track of software assets in an organized manner. Lyons, a dynamic and hard-driving executive, was anxious to start another company. He wanted to leverage his experience with reengineering to enter the rapidly expanding client/server market. Like Forte, Dynasty raised quite a bit of venture capital—$28 million in this case—and the company moved quickly to create a position in the second-generation client/server market.[9]

Dynasty gained a head start by purchasing some technology to help automate business processes as the anchor of its approach to client/server. Very much like Gupta Technologies, Dynasty prided itself on providing advanced object-oriented technology that, if implemented properly, could help its customers codify their business practices in software. Also very much like Gupta, it was complicated software requiring sophisticated programming knowledge. However, there were some very large companies that decided to take the risk and implement the software. Dynasty grew in part because of the momentum in the market and in part because the company was able to make the right connections to investors, large customers, the press, and industry analysts.[10]

Unlike Forte, Dynasty was not able to go public during the window of opportunity. It also refused offers to be acquired. However, after building a huge infrastructure to support its growing customer base, including setting up sales and support offices all over the world, the company wasn't able to make the type of money needed to continue to expand. At the same time, customers were growing impatient. These client/server systems were expensive to buy, complicated to build, and difficult to maintain. It was also difficult to find developers who had the skills to program a Dynasty system. By 1996, it was clear that momentum was waning. In the end, the company sold most of its assets to a European Investment firm called European Technology and Finance, which continues to maintain, sell, and support the software.

THE INEVITABILITY OF THE GOTCHA

Although innovation is imperative in transforming any market and moving any industry forward, risks and pitfalls are inevitable. Markets move in cycles, especially markets as fluid as technology. Each new invention and innovation opens up opportunities for entrepreneurs looking for opportunity. Typically, a combination of factors, rather than a single event, triggers an era of invention. Two primary factors that opened this opportunity in the client/server market were improvements in microprocessors and advances in software development. The new processors designed for the PC offered increasing amounts of power at a fraction of the cost of previous models. With this increased power, software developers gained the freedom to write software without worrying about running out of capacity. Therefore developers were free to make their products more graphical and more approachable than ever before. This new functionality could be combined with the minicomputer, which had also gone through a major transformation from a self-contained system that supported one business application to a way to manage complex applications. The minicomputer that Digital Equipment Corporation and Wang Laboratories had pioneered now became a "server"—a component in a new generation of systems.

The gotcha of the client/server era was that the technology simply wasn't ready to deal with the magnitude of the customers' needs. In gotcha markets what appears to be immediate success is the result of pent-up demand for something that will solve a difficult problem. But time and the maturation of technology prove that, although the concept was sound, the implementation was off base.

Lessons Learned

Lesson One: When a market is imploding, fix the flaws in your product or discover a market that needs what you have built. Unfortunately, often only in hindsight does it becomes apparent that a market is really just a way station on the path to the next, more sustainable technology or marketplace. If you find yourself in a gotcha market where you've invested in technology and that technology is failing to meet customer needs, take the best elements that your own technologists have designed and move them forward quickly. If this type of innovation doesn't exist inside the company, find a start-up that can help make the transition easier.

Lesson Two: Be objective about your own technology. Entrepreneurs tend to fall in love with their own products. They latch onto a product, idea, or opportunity and run fast—often without understanding where the flaws may be. Although passion is important, it is equally important to know where the problems are. If you can address problems quickly, you won't get swept away by a gotcha market.

Lesson Three: Keep it simple. One of the biggest problems for the companies that were transforming the landscape of client/server was the complexity of their technology. These companies built tools that required too much knowledge, too much work, and too much money. It is not always the most sophisticated or best technology that wins—rather, it is the technology that is good enough to get the job done.

As the seeds of change were sown in artificial intelligence, object-oriented technology, open systems, and the client/server market, the entrepreneurs who were smart enough to read the signals—pent-up customer demand, the falling prices of components, and the availability of financing—were the most likely to have initial success. But almost all first-generations technologies have the same gotcha: they are simply too immature to gain sustainability, and companies that invest all their resources in the first generation of a new technology are usually left with little to show for it. Lasting success usually comes slowly, so it is important to pay attention to where the technology is trending and to be flexible enough to move with it to avoid the fate of the gotcha.

As long as we are lucky we attribute it to our smartness;
our bad luck we give the gods credit for.
　　　　—Josh Billings, pen name of the humorist born
　　　　　　　Henry Wheller Shaw (1818–1885)

Chapter Eight

STANDING ON THE SHOULDERS OF PIONEERS

How Lessons Learned from the Past Pave the Way for New Technology

Momentous change does not happen overnight; it evolves over decades. Cloud computing and many other advances in technology have been built on the foundation of decades of experience and experimentation. Learning the lessons of earlier eras can pay huge dividends for entrepreneurs looking for new opportunities.

It should be clear by this point that no commercial technology becomes a success overnight. The most successful technology companies stand on the shoulders of the pioneers who came up with innovative concepts before the market was ready. Sometimes these inventors fail to achieve long-term success themselves because they are not savvy about the world of business. More often, the infrastructure hasn't been developed enough to support the technology. However, these pioneers do pave the way for lucky entrepreneurs who are able to leverage the lessons of the past when the market is ready, capitalizing on the availability of mature technology.

Even the smartest among us cannot forecast the impact of technology. There was a time when leaders of the mainframe market could not imagine that there would ever be a need for more than a few computers. There was huge skepticism surrounding graphical user interfaces and color screens for computers. In the early 1990s, few companies could imagine what a business would ever use the Internet for. There are thousands of examples of changes in technology that were once viewed as mere curiosities. Even the printing press was viewed by many as either dangerous or unimportant when it was invented.

It is almost impossible to predict the path a new technology idea will take. And it is abundantly clear that no life-changing innovation could pop into existence without relying on the knowledge and lessons learned from what came before. Rather, it is typically a combination of technology innovations, trial and error, and the ability to stand on the shoulders of pioneers that helps every successful entrepreneur achieve that success.

Cloud Computing

Technically, cloud computing automates many of the tedious tasks done in IT departments. In some ways it resembles the transformation that happened in banking when customers first gained the option of using an ATM to conduct their banking business rather than interacting directly with a teller. Likewise, cloud computing provides a self-service interface that allows customers to ask for the resources they need. This is possible because behind the scenes these tasks have been automated. The customer of a cloud service doesn't need to know where that computing resource is physically located or how it works—just as the banking customer doesn't know the details of how money is transferred and tracked. A cloud computing environment is set up so that the consumer of services can "rent" just as much of the computing resource as they need at the time they need it.

Cloud computing is one of those concepts that suddenly appeared, as though out of nowhere. It has become the biggest high-tech phenomenon since the advent of client/server computing and the commercial Internet. Cloud computing is not one single technology. In one form it enables customers to purchase extra computing resources to help them cope with traffic spikes. Why would they need extra computing resources? Take the example of Hallmark. On Valentine's Day 2005, more than a million customers logged in to Hallmark's website, causing it to crash several times.[1] Such incidents have led smart companies to use cloud services for times when they know there will be a demand for extra computing requirements. Without cloud computing services available as needed, these companies would have to purchase additional computers and other communications hardware and software for a single exceptional event. In addition, software developers can use a cloud system to rent out some room on a system to develop software before their employers decide whether the software should become a product. Again, the company can avoid spending vast sums of money on hardware and software for what might turn out to be a failed experiment. Some customers use cloud computing data centers to supplement their own data centers. Electronic mail, a necessary fact of corporate life, is an excellent example of a service that can be managed more economically in the cloud. Individuals, small and medium-sized companies, and even some very large ones are using cloud computing services like Google's Gmail, Microsoft Exchange, Lotus Notes, and Yahoo mail as a substitute for their own email systems.

Cloud computing in all its forms is transforming the computing landscape. Cloud computing built on the Internet in that it provides a communications platform for creating linkages between software elements. It is a new way of implementing business processes between partners and of managing relationships and computing resources. So cloud computing is about how you access power, how you organize your assets, how you control your intellectual property, whom you trust, and how you choose to change the way you conduct business.

Cloud computing is very much like the Internet market in its early days because it is not simply a technology movement; it touches consumers just as much as it touches complex businesses. Here are a couple of examples. Let's say you take hundreds, maybe thousands, of digital photos. No longer do you go to your own darkroom or send them to a lab for development. Rather, your photos remain in your camera or you transfer them onto a PC. But you want to show your photos to your friends and family. You can now subscribe to any of hundreds of services that enable you to store your pictures in a cloud—that is, in someone else's server in a data center. You tell your friends and family the link and your password, and now they all can look at the ten thousand pictures of your new puppy or your trip to Disney World.

The same concept applies in the world of commerce. For example, the typical hospital has hundreds of thousands of X-ray films stored in vast basement warrens, and a technician has to do a manual search to find an existing X-ray. If a patient happens to be traveling and an older X-ray is required for diagnostic purposes, a hospital might have to wait overnight while an X-ray film is mailed. And in extreme conditions, such as in a disaster area, there might be no easy way to move X-ray equipment into a remote site. But by using cloud computing in conjunction with advanced digital technology, X-ray images can be stored in a computer cloud and easily shared across town or across continents.

Cloud computing has extremely broad uses. It enables companies to use extra computing resources for a couple of hours or a couple of days and pay for only what they use, because it creates a simple way for the business user to go to an Internet browser and "order" more capacity, rather than relying on a complicated process established in a traditional IT department. It permits companies that used to purchase software directly to rely on infrastructure-as-a-service vendors to run the software for them. They simply lease an application over the Internet from the vendor. They can choose whether to lease the software one month at a time or for a year or two. The user doesn't have to update the application or back up the data—that is all part of the service.

Many innovative ideas and much technology underlie the business models created by such emerging leaders in the cloud market as Amazon.com, Google, and Facebook. Amazon.com provides customers with timed access to computing resources. When the customer is finished with the task, it no longer pays for the resource. Google has focused on building a platform that helps its partners build their own applications. Facebook uses the power of its half-billion members to sell advertising.

It is important to look at the origins of cloud computing, which, like all other important technologies, did not come out of nowhere, born of a company's inspiration to invent the future, but rather evolved. In reality, cloud computing is the beneficiary of three important innovations in the technology industry: time-sharing service bureaus, outsourcing providers, and managed service and application service providers. Let's take a closer look at each of these innovations.

Time-Sharing Service Bureaus

In the 1960s, John McCarthy, a computer science pioneer, suggested that the future evolution of computing would be as a utility—very much like the telephone systems.[2] He was indeed ahead of his time, but his prediction was correct. When McCarthy made this prediction, he was thinking about time-sharing. In the 1960s, the idea that multiple customers would be able to share a single computer to initiate their projects was revolutionary. Prior to the development of time-sharing, only the biggest companies in the world could afford their own systems. If a smaller company needed computing resources, it had to contact the owner of a large system and request that the larger company execute its project. Time-sharing was different; the customer would have a computer terminal that was connected through a communications link to a service bureau (a commercial organization that ran complex applications for its customers). The customer now had the freedom to use these computer resources without the expense of purchasing the system. Unfortunately for the service bureau business, as the market for computers expanded, prices began to drop. In addition, as more and more companies began to automate, the cost of computer resources became more affordable and the service bureaus were no longer competitive.

Outsourcing Providers

In the 1980s, as emerging and more agile companies began to challenge the supremacy of traditional corporations, it became clear that something would have to change. These once-powerful companies knew that, if they were going to survive in the long term, they would have to transform their business practices. Consultants challenged these companies to understand what their core competencies were and then to streamline their business practices. Many of these consultants told their clients that information technology was a resource that they shouldn't be managing themselves. They urged clients to hire outside firms with specialized skills that could run information technology and data centers as an efficient business. These outsourcing providers simply took over the entire data center operation, so that the company no longer had any control of its technology assets.

Managed Service Providers and Application Service Providers

One of the biggest trends of the 1990s was the development of the managed service provider and the application service provider.

These are companies that take over the tasks of running applications or managing how those applications perform so that companies don't have to do these tasks within their own organizations. Managed service providers evolved from the outsourcing model. Whereas an outsourcer would take over the entire data center, the managed service provider would take over one aspect of a company's IT requirements. For example, a customer might have asked it to operate a computer network or a set of hardware assets that needed to be managed differently from the rest of the data center.

The application service provider was also a form of outsourcing. However, application service providers specialized in operating a specific application for a customer. Managed service providers came to prominence in the mid-1990s during the height of the dot-com era. Dot-com companies found it difficult to support the growing computing requirements of their customers, so they turned to managed service providers for help. Managed service providers enabled these companies to present a well-managed computing environment to their customers and provided them with space in a climate-controlled and secure data center equipped with the latest communications capability—namely, extra power supplies in case of a power outage. The dot-com companies brought their own computers and their own software to the managed service provider, who would then provide what some called "ping, pipe, and power" (*ping* meaning the Internet, *pipe* meaning the communications backbone, and *power* as in electricity). Over time, these managed service providers added new offerings, such as security services. These foundational services, developed by managed service providers, are now incorporated as foundational services in cloud computing environments.

Ten years later, there are no application service providers; rather, the concept morphed into cloud computing. Customers want to achieve the same business goals today with cloud computing as they did with application service providers, but the technology has matured significantly, so the dreams of these early innovators are becoming much more solid and predictable as we move further into the twenty-first century.

Cloud computing would not have been possible without the interim technology innovations that preceded it. Whether we are talking about the invention of the Internet itself as a U.S. Defense Department funded project in 1969, or the advent of application service providers, all of these approaches had to evolve before we could begin to think about a market for commercial-grade computing based on the ability to predictably manage these resources. But because of these past innovations, thousands of companies began building innovative businesses based on cloud computing.

SALESFORCE.COM

One such company that built upon the experience of others is saleseforce.com. Salesforce.com is a software-as-a-service vendor that provides a way for companies to manage and analyze data about their customer and prospects. A company that needs to track what products and services customers are buying, what stage a salesperson is in terms of working with prospects, and so on can use the packaged implementation of this application from salesforce .com to do so. However, rather than buying the software and implementing inside a data center, the customer buys a license for each user who will need to access the software. The software itself resides inside salesforce.com's data centers. Salesforce.com manages all the software updates directly and backs up the information. Salesforce.com uses a technology approach called "multi-tenancy," which means that data from each of its customers is stored in containers separate from other companies' data.

Salesforce.com has succeeded because it was lucky enough to be in the right place at the right time. But it also had the advantage of understanding the mistakes of the early sales automation software market and was smart enough to learn from companies that had tried to sell software as a service in the past. In addition, salesforce .com hit the market right before cloud computing became a reality. Cofounder Marc Benioff grew up in the computer industry, spending the first thirteen years of his career at Oracle. Although his early career appeared to be fairly conventional, Benioff was a creative thinker as well as a great showman. Benioff also had the good fortune of being able to learn many lessons from the new generation of the packaged software market that was beginning to thrive in the 1990s. Most important, Benioff was smart enough to build upon the experiences of sales automation software companies like PeopleSoft, ACT, and Siebel Systems.

Lessons from Siebel Systems

There had always been packaged software to handle business tasks like accounting and manufacturing, but in the 1990s the ability to automate sales and marketing was relatively new. Hundreds of companies saw the opportunity to sell software to the millions of sales personnel and marketing managers who previously had to rely on paper to manage prospects and customers. With the advent of client/server computing, the opportunities began to explode. It was clear that if a company could sell an application to hundreds or thousands of salespeople, the potential revenue was immense. Therefore it was not surprising that hundreds of start-ups entered this market. While many of these companies are long forgotten, a few managed to establish significant market share and revenue growth. One of those companies was Siebel Systems, founded in 1993 by Tom Siebel and Patricia House, two Oracle executives.

Many of the early sales force automation systems had given customers only the capability to manage basic lists of customers and prospects, without the ability to analyze that data. However, companies like Siebel Systems created a more comprehensive approach to sales management. The Siebel development team focused on creating software that would allow the sales team to integrate information about customers and prospects and then analyze this information based on opportunities, competitive threats, and trends. To do this, the company had to focus on creating software that would support not just a single sales representative, but an entire sales organization. Therefore the software needed lots of functionality to support many different sales processes. It also needed to support large teams across the globe, and in order to do this it had to understand different pricing models based on different languages and different currencies. It also had to allow sales leaders to customize the business process, based on how the company managed its sales efforts.[3]

Siebel released its system to the market in 1994 with a price of as much as $6,500 per user. Even at this price, there was so much pent-up demand that the company did extremely well. It landed brand name accounts like Charles Schwab, Cisco, and Anderson Consulting. One year later, the company had $8 million in revenue and continued to innovate. It added an enterprise version of the software that now included more management, reporting, and forecasting capabilities. By 1996, revenue had swelled to $39 million and the company went public. As a public company with the demands to continue to grow revenue, the company began making acquisitions, aiming to add Internet enablement or specific market knowledge. By the end of the decade, the company also expanded into adjacent markets such as customer relationship management. In subsequent years, Siebel continued to make significant acquisitions, and by the year 2000 the company had reached $1.8 billion in revenue.

Despite its position in the Customer Relationship Management (CRM) market, however, all was not going well with Siebel. Siebel and its competitors spent huge amounts of time and money adding more and more capability to the software, but unfortunately, this made it increasingly difficult to use. When many companies that had purchased the software found their sales and marketing teams unable to use it, they began wondering why they had spent so much money for so little return. Making matters worse for these emerging companies, large established players like Oracle and SAP were starting to build software to compete with the upstarts. Even if the functionality of these products was not as compelling, these bigger companies had the advantage of their long-term relationships with customers. They could promise better-integrated support and management, and they could assure the customer that the company would be around for the long term. In 2005, Oracle, which had decided to create a major business consolidating the packaged software market, purchased Siebel Systems for $5.8 billion.[4]

Salesforce.com Is Born

In 1999, around the same time that Siebel was flying high, Marc Benioff left Oracle to found salesforce.com.[5] Benioff had the advantage of having participated in many aspects of Oracle's business. He saw the incredible successes that Oracle achieved by focusing its efforts on executing well on its business model. He also saw what happened when Oracle tried to compete with upstarts like Powersoft in the graphical development market. At that time, Oracle had designed a standalone graphical development tool designed to work like Powersoft. However, it was not differentiated enough to make either Oracle's or Powersoft's customers switch their allegiance. Also, its graphical development tool could not work with Oracle's existing software development environments, nor could it interoperate with Powersoft's environment. These experiences taught Benioff an important lesson when he started his own venture: for customers to switch from what they are comfortable with, there has to be a compelling business reason.

It might have been safer for Benioff to remain at Oracle and create new offerings within the existing structure. But in some ways it is more liberating to start with a clean slate. When entrepreneurs build a company from scratch, they are not faced with existing customers who prefer to stay with the status quo and add incremental functionality to an existing system. There are no competing factions within a new company. Entrepreneurs creating new enterprises can therefore give their creativity free rein to solve problems that incumbent market leaders were unable to address.

Of course, the blank slate creates challenges as well as opportunities. What are the unsolved customer problems in the market with no obvious solution? How can you convince skeptical potential investors that this is the one idea that will make them rich? How do you convince potential customers that it is safe to take a risk on a company with few customers, little revenue, and big competitors?

When Marc Benioff decided to strike out on his own, he faced all of these questions, but he also had a few strategic advantages. He was well known in the computer industry because of his years at Oracle. He had made enough money at Oracle that he didn't have to worry initially about raising early capital. And he was lucky too—he picked the customer relationship management (CRM) market just as customers were beginning to be frustrated by cumbersome and difficult software solutions. It would be a few years before the industry accepted the idea of allowing a software-as-a-service vendor to control customer management for its clients, but by combining the mature CRM market with a new cloud computing delivery model, Benioff was ready when customers were willing to take a risk on what he was selling.

Benioff decided to focus his energy on innovating how a CRM system could be redesigned, and he managed to solve many of the problems with existing CRM products. The notion of offering software as a service wasn't new. For example, ADP—a human resources, payroll, tax and benefit services company founded in

1949—began offering Internet-based services in 2003, and after only eight years the company had revenues of $9 billion and was supporting 570,000 clients. And there were already hundreds of managed service providers operating applications for their customers. So Benioff had models of both success and failure to guide him. Even more important, he had a clear vision of where he wanted to go and the audacity to take big risks to get there.

It is noteworthy that when Benioff founded salesforce.com in 1999, the company didn't start with a massive applications infrastructure for sales or marketing automation.[6] What it had was a very simple contact management system on the Web that was available to anyone willing to try it at no cost. Although it wasn't unusual for a company to offer free software, there was a difference in salesforce .com's strategy. Many of the early dot-com companies offered free technology without any clear plan for making money. Benioff, in contrast, looked beyond the initial free product. His initial offering was merely a test to determine potential customers' preferences. His long-term strategy was to create a platform out of this initial trial. He was targeting the big players in the sales and marketing automation market.

A New Approach to Software

By the end of the 1990s, the potential problems for early market leaders like Siebel were starting to become apparent to customers and competitors. In highly competitive markets, companies continue to expand functionality in order to sell more modules to existing customers as well as to attract new ones. The result is not surprising—the software becomes more and more difficult to navigate and implement. But ironically, this complexity does not become as big a negative as one might imagine. Systems integration firms see the enormous opportunity for helping customers implement complex systems, and a symbiotic relationship develops.

Benioff was beginning to see the toll that this complexity was taking on customers. A trickle of articles pointed out what was happening with these massive systems: either they were not being implemented by customers or sales personnel were refusing to use them. Salesforce .com was able to learn the important lesson of the problems created by too much complexity. Therefore, when the company designed its product it proposed to take the opposite tack. It would make the product more approachable. It would take away the burden of having to set up and customize the software.

The opening salvo in salesforce.com's strategy was to turn the market upside down by sowing seeds of doubt about the traditional approach to selling software. But it is important to recognize that Benioff didn't hatch his strategy by sitting in a room alone. He had a lot of help. For example, he sought out advice from experienced leaders, including Larry Ellison, CEO of Oracle; Michael Dell, CEO of Dell Inc.; and Craig Conway, former CEO of PeopleSoft. Smart entrepreneurs pay close attention to what both successful and failed leaders have to teach them. Benioff partnered with Rick Bennett, a marketing entrepreneur who had helped Larry Ellison and many other software companies with their marketing campaigns. The resulting marketing campaign was brilliant. Rather than promoting the platform's superiority to conventional software, salesforce.com proclaimed that it wasn't even selling software. Its message was basically that software was dead, replaced by this new method of providing customer value. The symbol—the word "software" with a slash through it—became the company's calling card. Rather than focusing on the features of its products, it focused on its customers' pain. Installing and using software is often cumbersome, expensive, and time-consuming. Salesforce.com promised to make all of that pain go away.

Why was this campaign so important? When you have a start-up that is taking on powerful incumbents, it is impossible to simply point to more or better functionality. Too many emerging companies try to compete by pointing out that their technology is much more sophisticated than existing products. Unfortunately, even if this claim is true, new innovation is often too complicated for customers to understand. And that's assuming the customer even has the inclination to try to understand. One of the key principles of effective marketing is that customers will not buy something that they don't understand. Salesforce.com understood this. It did not try to convince customers that its products had better functions; rather, it told customers that there was a simpler way to get the job done with less pain and less cost. In other words, they could get the benefits they needed to manage their sales force without the problems of enterprise software. Thus salesforce.com had turned the conversation away from features and functions to a discussion of customer pain and solutions.

So the big question for someone like Benioff, looking to turn a market upside down, was this: Would customers be willing to risk moving away from the software model that they had become comfortable with over the previous fifty years?

Convincing Customers to Adopt

During salesforce.com's early years, it wasn't at all clear that prospective customers would be willing to take that risk and turn their sales or marketing automation process over to a software-as-a-service company. The risks were real. Where would the software be stored? Could someone without authorization access key customer information? What would happen if the company went out of business? What if there were flaws in the product? This model—having a vendor simply rent access to an application—was understandably scary to large enterprises. These companies were accustomed to owning a license to the software they relied on to run their businesses.

While these large companies were unwilling to move forward, the individual business units within both large companies and small ones were not afraid of the idea of software as a service. Departments of large companies that were frustrated by the inability of their IT organizations to give them the type of easy access to applications they needed, and small companies that wanted to avoid spending money on computing infrastructure, were eager to adopt software as a service. These two constituents were salesforce.com's first customers. However, to be truly successful, salesforce.com needed the large companies to accept the cloud model. Therefore the company nurtured these departmental customers that had begun slowly experimenting with salesforce.com.

This is similar to what happened when personal computers were first introduced into large corporations. While the centralized IT department was unconvinced that PCs would be useful, business units purchased them anyway. In the long run IT management was forced to change its policy and adopt the PC as a departmental standard. Likewise, with salesforce.com, not only was centralized IT opposed to software as a service, but it wasn't even aware that it was being used widely. It was easy and inexpensive to get started: no installation of software and no systems integrator knocking on the door. Within a short period of time, this process became common-place. By the time the centralized IT organization discovered that hundreds of divisional sales professionals were happily using the Salesforce Software Environment, it was impossible to shut it down.

Had salesforce.com simply offered a hosted version of CRM software, it would not have distinguished itself in the market. Many entrepreneurs are technologists first and salespeople second. With Benioff, the sales and marketing process was as important as the technology. Indeed, salesforce.com transformed the process of convincing customers to adopt technology quickly. A customer could start with a free personal copy of Salesforce (with somewhat limited features) to get familiar with the software. Gaining access to all the functions salesforce.com offered required an upgrade to the enterprise version. Salesforce also emphasized customer support. It became very apparent from the experience of the early application service providers that if customers did not start using the product quickly, they would simply stop paying. For a company that relied on customers willing to commit on a monthly or yearly basis, making the customer dependent on the system was critical.

But excellent customer support isn't enough to transform a company from an interesting start-up to a powerhouse. Trust is a necessary component of success. Customers are hesitant to invest heavily in time, training, money, and reputation if the vendor doesn't have long-term viability. Having watched his mentor, Oracle founder Larry Ellison, for more than a decade, Benioff had learned important lessons and techniques. Being good isn't enough; successful companies are maniacally driven. To succeed, Benioff knew he would have to engage in guerrilla marketing and use unconventional tactics to gain traction.

Benioff's guerrilla marketing consisted of using his personal and professional relationships, gained through his years at Oracle and his close relationship with Ellison, to learn how to create a software company that could scale. He also leveraged his relationships with well-known CEOs of companies like Intel and Cisco, getting both companies to adopt salesforce.com internally and to publically endorse the product as well. He actively courted journalists and analysts, inviting them to intimate events with high-profile customers and prospects. As a result, salesforce.com received a huge amount of media attention. Journalists wrote articles about this emerging company; industry analysts gave the company and its approach the seal of approval. As salesforce.com grew and started holding conferences, Benioff paid all expenses for influential opinion makers to attend his events. Few emerging companies have the clout to convince top analysts and industry leaders to drop everything to attend their conferences. With

Benioff's connections and money, he convinced executives to flock to his meetings. Through these gatherings, Salesforce impressed many influential analysts. Benioff invited them to attend dinners at well-known restaurants with thirty or forty executives of major corporations who were using his technology. Sure, an analyst needs to maintain objectivity, but it is hard not to be impressed when top executives surround you and tout the products of the sponsoring company. And, of course, you are flattered to have been invited.

Building an Ecosystem

Salesforce.com also followed another tried and true approach to bringing products to market—building a successful ecosystem. An ecosystem is a group of partners that use the company's platform to expand into new markets. For example, salesforce.com established a partner program called AppExchange, a program that provides a sales channel for partners who build their own software offerings using salesforce.com's underlying software infrastructure. Therefore, a devoted customer can find adjacent software that works easily with salesforce.com's functionality, such as sales compensation or data management. When it promotes another company's products, salesforce.com takes a percentage of the revenue and increases its lock on customers. If customers can get more and more of the functionality they need by sticking with the company, that increases its long-term viability.

Apple Inc. has taken the same approach with its online iTunes and its App Store; Google has done much the same thing with Google App Engine and its Android wireless operating system. For generations, enterprise software vendors have created partner and channel marketing programs to create tight relationships that spread their functionality well beyond the bounds of their own product offerings. Even online gaming software companies have been able to create an ecosystem of partners. Cloud computing and the Internet simply increase the speed and effectiveness of such partnering.

Remaining Competitive

Since 2009, salesforce.com has exceeded $1 billion in revenue. With such success come risks. A company that reaches these heights has a virtual target on its back. Companies big and small look at the business model and begin to copy it. Companies like Oracle, IBM, Intuit, and hundreds of others are not standing idly by. They are reinventing their own products to leverage the cloud market. New companies are taking the lessons learned and coming up with competing products. SugarCRM is an open source–based software-as-a-service CRM company that offers a less expensive alternative to Salesforce. In addition, another open source competitor is Zoho, an India-based software-as-a-service company.[7] Zoho has duplicated the functionality in salesforce.com's offerings with an open source model. It has developed hundreds of modules of functionality, such as invoicing, online chat, and online meetings, as well as integration with partners' products, such as Intuit's QuickBooks accounting software. With the path blazed by salesforce.com, it doesn't have to convince potential customers about the safety of the software-as-a-service model. It can simply offer similar functionality at a lower cost. For example, for companies that support fewer than five salespeople, the software is free. The company begins charging as the amount of data and complexity of the sales model increases. Venture capitalists who feared the software-as-a-service model a decade ago are jumping on board and funding hundreds of start-ups. Salesforce.com can't ignore the threats. Therefore the company continues to increase its strategic partnerships with everyone from Google to VMware to Informatica. It will continue to add functionality to stay a step ahead of its competitors. This won't be easy, and there is no way to predict whether a few years from now another start-up will come up with a product that challenges its position.

Secrets of Success

The techniques employed by salesforce.com have worked, and the company has done a lot of things right. Despite its claim that it does not sell software, it created a software platform for sales forces and marketing organizations that has many of the capabilities of traditional enterprise software. However, because the company's business model is predicated on periodic subscription renewals, it had to create a platform that was easy to use. That has worked well. Many businesses had found that traditional sales automation products were simply too cumbersome for the sales force to use. Early market leaders like Siebel expanded their functionality so much that the software became more and more difficult to navigate and implement, and many companies simply surrendered when their salespeople refused to use the products. The secret to salesforce.com's initial success was that its technology was easy to get started with and easy to use. Large companies that were initially resistant to the idea of software as a service in the cloud have changed their tune. The differences in implementation costs and usage patterns have been game changers. It is an important lesson—if you solve complex problems with minimal pain, the customers will follow.

Salesforce.com has become a formidable company in cloud computing. It smartly combined the need to manage sales information with a more flexible technology than had previously been available. It also added new products that could work hand in hand with sales information offerings. Salesforce.com also convinced other software companies to build their software solutions on top of the salesforce.com cloud environment. The company was also lucky in many ways; it was able to take advantage of the early experiments offered by the application service providers and the managed service providers. And by the time salesforce.com had a fully operational system that it was beginning to offer as a service, the dot-com meltdown had already happened. Salesforce.com was able to learn important lessons about how to scale a business based on a long-term vision—a lesson that the dot-com companies failed to understand. Benioff also had the timing right. The cloud computing market was about to become a major market force just as he was creating his business model. Perhaps, if Benioff had left Oracle a few years earlier, he would have been caught up in the same insanity as the rest of the dot-com market and would have failed. But, as it happened, he learned from the mistakes of others who preceded him and has led his company to success.

Lessons Learned

Lesson One: Watch for customer pain in established markets. It is very hard to win in a market where you have to start from scratch. If you can transform an existing market with a new approach, you have a better chance of succeeding.

Lesson Two: Learn from the successes and failures of earlier markets. There is no such thing as a technology market that comes out of nowhere. Salesforce.com had the luck to come after and learn from application service providers and managed service providers who had created the market that would become software as a service and cloud computing. Therefore it is important to take advantage of the experience of previous experiments.

Lesson Three: Overcome customer fear. Salesforce.com's earliest customers were very small companies. These companies were more fearful of having to support hardware than of allowing an application to run in the cloud. Overcoming objections of larger companies is very difficult. Patience and persistence pay off.

Lesson Four: Develop a great marketing platform for your technology. It isn't enough to develop sophisticated technology. Great marketing and great relationships often trump great technology. Winning the support of market influencers pays huge dividends.

Salesforce.com was lucky enough to start in its business just as cloud computing was beginning to take shape as an important market. However, luck is never enough. Salesforce.com was smart enough to be able to leverage the experiments, the successes, and the failures of many earlier markets: the CRM market, the application service provider market, and the managed service provider markets. To achieve success, it is important to build on the innovations of pioneers.

I've found that luck is quite predictable. If you want more luck, take more chances. Be more active. Show up more often.

—Brian Tracy, training consultant

Chapter Nine

THE SILVER BULLET SYNDROME

Beware of Solutions That Appear
Too Good to Be True

Emerging technology markets provide huge opportunities for enterprising entrepreneurs. The excitement is contagious and can turn traditional technology markets upside down. Entrepreneurs are looking for instant fame and fortune, venture capitalists are looking for returns on investment, and customers are looking for quick solutions, or "silver bullets." But these silver bullet markets fade as quickly as they start. When you are caught up in one of these whirlwinds, make sure you remain levelheaded, and use the market momentum to prepare for the future.

A silver bullet is the legendary ammunition guaranteed to kill a vampire. One simple solution and your vampire problems are solved. Although there are no vampires (that I know of) in the technology market, there are plenty of inventions and products that offer customers quick solutions and promise unattainable results. Unfortunately, when it comes to technology, there is usually no one answer, cure-all, or quick fix, and when the technology industry promises a silver bullet that will solve customers' problems quickly and easily, you can bet it will be far more complicated than promised.

The term "no silver bullet" was used in the context of technology and software in a paper written by Fred Brooks, author of *The Mythical Man-Month,* and a computer scientist who managed the development of IBM's most successful mainframe project, the System/360 and its operating system. In a widely read article about silver bullets, first published in *Computer* magazine in 1987, Brooks states, ". . . as we look to the horizon of a decade hence, we see no silver bullets. There is no single development, in either technology or in management technique, that by itself promises even one order-of-magnitude improvement in productivity, in reliability, in simplicity . . ."[1]

Emerging technologies are about hope, promise, and solving the seemingly unsolvable. When big ideas take hold, they capture the imaginations of inventors, venture capitalists, marketers, and customers. However, the world of technology is filled with the wrecks of products that promised to change the world. Some things never change: if something seems too good to be true, it usually is. Technology companies that are built on a promise rather than a strong foundation usually fail miserably.

Innovative technology is a thread that runs through human history. The common denominator of innovations is that they are all, well, innovative; they are different from what has come before. They take a seemingly unsolvable problem and propose a solution. Sure, there have been some innovations that followed through on their potential. Take the loom, invented in 1804 by Joseph Marie Jacquard. It automated the process of manufacturing textiles by transforming complex fabric patterns into a series of punched cards. Or the steam engine, invented by James Watts in 1776, which was key to initiating the Industrial Revolution. Or the electric light bulb that was perfected by Thomas Edison in 1879 and transformed the number of hours people could work and what they could do with their free time. Each of these inventions transformed not only a particular industry but also society itself. Yet for every successful invention there have been thousands of other inventions that offered huge promise but never made it off the drawing board. When was the last time you saw an ad for an inexpensive personal flying machines? Or a nuclear-powered vacuum cleaner, predicted in 1955? Or a personal submarine, predicted in 1900? How about a fancy hotel built under an ocean? Yet in the early twentieth century it was predicted that these and other technologies would transform the way we live forever.

Reality rarely keeps up with the fantasy of how a compelling and innovative technology will change life as we know it. In reality, solutions are complicated, incremental, and expensive, and customers are impatient when it comes to learning and implementing new technology. The great thing about a silver bullet is that if you deploy one to handle your vampire problem, it is failsafe. Your problem is solved! Alas, in the world of technology innovation, solutions are not so simple. Companies spend huge amounts of time and money trying to find answers to problems and even more trying to figure out how to entice customers to use their technology. And in the process of trying to persuade customers to use their products, they'll often promise a silver bullet, but deliver something that doesn't live up to expectations.

There is a predictable trajectory for technology trends. A new technology is developed based on engineering or computer science principles. It is nurtured by a few technical gurus who begin to collaborate on this emerging technology. Fast-forward a few years, or sometimes as much as a decade or more, and the first commercial products appear. These early innovative products catch the attention of large companies that want to experiment with any technology that might, in the future, be a game changer. If that company can gain early experience with an important emerging technology and use it to gain competitive advantage, it is worth the risk. Often these experiments aren't successful. But once in a while they catch on. The ecosystem takes over. These large customers continue to buy, and the revenue of these early adopters begins to grow. Now the market starts to pay attention. *Maybe there is money to be made in this new technology.* Now the venture capitalists enter the fray. They begin funding companies started by those same technologists who designed the technology in the first place, plus a lot of other technologists who see the potential. Large, established companies also recognize the potential and use their marketing might to position themselves for the new market. They instruct their internal development staff to work on building comparable technology. Many established companies don't even wait until the products are completed before proclaiming leadership in the new market.

What happens next is also predictable. Customers get caught up in the excitement surrounding the new market. They don't want their companies to be left out. But there is a problem. They do not understand exactly what the technology does, how it works, or how it will benefit their organizations. Their CEOs see articles in business magazines about the importance of a new trend, and they want to know how the company plans to respond to this opportunity.

At this stage, the education process begins. Seminars, conferences, and vendor-sponsored events spring up everywhere to educate customers about the new technology. Hundreds of product companies start up. Some companies are well-funded by known industry luminaries or venture capitalists; others are founded by technologists with a germ of an idea. Many of the entrepreneurs, hoping to take advantage of the hype, will name their companies after the technology trend. The market begins to explode. Market research firms confirm that within the next five years the market will be worth billions of dollars. And now the true silver bullet marketing begins. *This new technology is powerful and will transform the value of the various industries it serves forever. Customers will increase their profitability; their own customers will be more satisfied; their own employees will be more productive.*

Customers are always eager to purchase technology that will make a difference and provide a competitive advantage. And many of these emerging vendors, as well as their more mature competitors, don't want to inform these eager buyers that the technology is still immature. In reality, most important technologies require a long-term commitment on the part of customers. They have to invest time, money, and training to get results—and results don't come quickly. That silver bullet turns out to be more difficult to implement and integrate into a business than the vendor had predicted. If the customer is lucky, the product helps solve a tricky problem. Sometimes the technology helps one company gain a competitive advantage. These success stories begin to circulate in the market. The market continues to evolve and expand.

Usually, just as customers begin to get real benefit from the emerging technologies, the market changes. Now the hard work begins. Customers no longer talk about the wonders of the technology; they have moved into the implementation phase, and when they are grinding away at their day-to-day work, there is little glamour. The excitement is gone. During this phase, the market is typically declared dead. No technology can ever live up to its hype. When customers come to terms with the technology and its complexity, it becomes clear that there is no silver bullet. Also, many of these innovations are immature; they are more difficult to use and cost more to implement than anyone had anticipated. New innovative technologies are risky, so failures are inevitable. There is an ongoing debate among shapers of opinion as to whether this technology will truly have an impact on the future. Suddenly no one wants to talk about the new market anymore.

But the biggest irony of all is that the innovative technology is far from dead. It has simply moved beyond the hype. The hard work begins when the hype cycle ends. Developers actually use the technology to accomplish real results, albeit not always the ones promised by the vendors selling the technology. The technology continues to provide some key benefits to customers, and long after the market hype goes away it morphs into a new generation of technology. Silver bullets are important because they often initiate innovative new technologies that will become important commercial products years later. The hype is equally important, because it forces vendors and investors to create new offerings and push the technology well beyond its origins. Without the educational process that is part of the silver bullet phase, customers would not be able to change their businesses.

Dynamic technology markets always seem to be in some sort of silver bullet phase. In mature markets, on the other hand, where there is little innovation, there are few silver bullets and little excitement. The cycles have to take place if technology is to move from the conceptualization stage to maturity. However, there are some technologies that reach maturity earlier than others. It is instructive to look at some of the silver bullets that have become the fabric of innovation today. Some we don't even think of as innovations anymore, because they are deeply embedded in everything we do.

THE INTERNET

Some of the technology industry's most significant silver bullets had their origin in the Internet. This decades-old but solid technology emerged commercially only in the late 1990s. The early products that leveraged the Internet as a foundation for their products were intended to create instant electronic commerce sites that would attract millions of customers and generate massive revenue overnight. During its first decade, many entrepreneurs wrongly assumed that the Internet itself was a market. But as the dot-com bubble burst, it became clear that the Internet was an enabling technology, driving and fueling a huge number of innovative products. We now take it for granted that there is a ubiquitous platform that fuels everything from Facebook to electronic commerce.

ARTIFICIAL INTELLIGENCE

In the 1980s another incredibly popular silver bullet took the market by storm. Artificial intelligence was implemented commercially in the form of automated expert systems designed to incorporate a specific set of rules into software to avoid manual programming. These systems offered the promise of enabling machines to replace routine human functions. For example, thanks to AI, people would no longer have to clean their homes or manage their finances. Robots would perform hundreds of mundane tasks. There were plenty of fears about how much our lives might change when we no longer had to think for ourselves. Companies in a myriad of industries took a look at artificial intelligence. For example, if artificial intelligence could be applied to the insurance industry, human activities could be analyzed by programs that would be able to easily calculate the risks of insuring an individual piece of property. At the same time that IT and business leaders were starting to learn about this innovation, venture capitalists and entrepreneurs began to invest in commercial products and companies to take advantage of this potential break-through. Companies including Mathematica, Symbolics, Paladin, IntelliCorp, Teknowledge, and GoldHill all introduced expert systems-based products. All of these companies designed their own hardware systems to deliver applications intended to help with everything from geological exploration to financial decision making to providing medical advice.

But, as often happens, companies who bought these early systems discovered the truth: there aren't any easy solutions to complex problems, and complex solutions are very expensive. Companies that purchased these systems actually had to program and input a lot of their own knowledge in order to make them operable. It was a difficult task and required years of research and planning. The promise of effortless progress, whereby the system would learn from prior experience and continue to evolve, never came to pass. Although customers were intrigued by the promise of artificial intelligence, they refused to purchase systems that would cost too much money and take too long to implement. These expert systems vendors simply could not survive.

However, the technology developed by these vendors did survive. Once expert system technology could be implemented on inexpensive hardware, new companies emerged that used the technology concepts to build solutions. For example, some were able to create "expert systems" whereby subject matter experts would input their understanding of the best practices in a specific industry into software. Customers would be able to transform that system by adding their own knowledge and the peculiarities of their companies. Today, expert system technology is embedded in most technology solutions. However, it was never a huge standalone market.

Artificial Intelligence has also had a huge impact on industry. Everything from a kitchen toaster to a data center uses "fuzzy" logic. Fuzzy logic uses mathematical techniques to understand the contextual relationships between situations. For example, if you can combine information about how fast your car is traveling with information about how far in front of you another car is, the system can deduce when you should put on your brakes in order to avoid a collision. In fact, many cars currently on the market already include such a system, helping to avoid accidents and making it easier to park.

OBJECT ORIENTATION

Object orientation is another innovation that failed to live up to its initial hype. Like other silver bullets, it was an important concept that is now widely used as the underpinning of a generation of products and technologies. As described earlier, the object orientation programming technique was developed in the 1950s and 1960s as a way of making programming more streamlined.[2] It was intended to enable programmers to focus on creating modular components that were very precise and could be more easily reused in different situations. By the 1980s, the commercial market was beginning to conclude that this sophisticated approach could be applied to emerging applications to revolutionize the way software was built. During this phase, hundreds of new languages and new applications emerged. IT organizations, seeing the potential power, began to study the technical intricacies of object orientation. Hundreds of companies entered the market, focused completely on the ability to reuse programs for many different situations. If these programs could be reused in a variety of situations, it would be easy for business people to connect programs so they could create their own applications without needing the help of specialized programmers.

There was plenty of hype and excitement about the object-oriented software development market in the late 1980s. Some pundits predicted that object-oriented technology would literally turn software development into the equivalent of the factory production assembly line. In fact, in 1988, Red Herring, a technology business magazine, predicted that "end users will be able to put software components together rapidly to create cheap, powerful, customizable, easy-to-use applications that are nearly maintenance free. Those applications will allow users intuitively to store, retrieve, and manipulate complex datatypes distributed over virtual networks. Large corporations will seamlessly incorporate multimedia and complex documents and images into their core mission-critical information systems . . . "[3]

The same article cited a Gartner Group survey predicting that by 1998, three out of every four large corporations would deploy object-oriented mission-critical applications. There were hundreds of companies, many of which went public, based on the explosion of interest in object-oriented technology. Companies like ParcPlace, Digitalk, Versant, Object Design, Objectivity, and Ontos became the darlings of the market. At the same time, industry leaders such as Microsoft, IBM, and Oracle began introducing products and partnerships to take advantage of this emerging market.

TALIGENT: A VICTIM OF THE SILVER BULLET

The story of the birth and death of a company called Taligent explains both the excitement and the disappointment of the object orientation silver bullet market.[4] In the early 1990s IBM and Apple began a collaboration with an emerging technology company called Metaphor Computer Systems.

Metaphor Computer Systems, a spinoff of Xerox's famous research and development laboratory called Xerox PARC, was a start-up that built an innovative object-oriented system in 1982. The goal of Metaphor Computer Systems was to transform the way the personal computer was designed and operated. The Metaphor system was a workstation that included a database, a graphical user interface, and built-in communications software. All the hardware and software elements were integrated. Each element was designed so that it could automatically communicate with any other element in the system. Because of these characteristics, Metaphor began attracting some very large customers that liked to experiment with innovative technology. Large customers like Procter & Gamble were demanding more support than the fledgling start-up could offer. Therefore Metaphor approached IBM, which was its hardware partner. IBM made an investment in the company in 1988.

By 1990, the market for object-oriented technology was heating up. IBM was intrigued by the idea of leveraging the Metaphor technology to create new products to compete in this emerging market. Metaphor would separate its software from its hardware, and the new product would not be tied to any single hardware platform.[5] The two companies established a new company called Patriot Partners to focus on developing object-oriented technology for personal computers. The new company would require several years before it could bring commercial products to market.

Just as Patriot Partners was getting off the ground, Apple computer approached IBM about partnering. During the early 1990s, Apple was having trouble attracting the attention of corporate buyers, who still saw Apple as a platform for individual rather than corporate use. Apple needed IBM's credibility with major accounts. IBM, on the other hand, needed Apple's experience making easy-to-use systems. Apple contributed its next-generation object-oriented operating system, called Pink. The collaboration between IBM and Apple was significant for three reasons. First, it meant that IBM believed that the object-oriented market was important and was willing to invest in a big way. Second, it signaled that Apple wanted to be a player in the enterprise. Third, it meant that the IBM and Microsoft partnership, based on a new object-oriented operating system called OS/2, was faltering.

The partnership now took a new direction. Metaphor, the original partner, was acquired by IBM, and IBM and Apple created a new company called Taligent to execute on the partnership. Taligent's aim was to create a software platform that would be object oriented from the operating system up to the applications development software. It would allow programmers to more easily create components of code that could work on any hardware platform without recoding—a necessary practice in previous generations of software. Although this is a well-accepted best practice today, it was considered revolutionary at the beginning of the 1990s.

As an independent company supported by its sponsors (by that time Hewlett Packard had joined), Taligent by 1994 employed more than 170 people.[6] IBM and Apple saw the potential power of creating technology that would cater to a marketplace for software components that were designed to work together out of the box. But it was simply too early. The object-oriented operating system and languages were not fully mature, and it was an uphill battle to implement this new approach to software design. Development was slow, and by the following year it became clear that the object-oriented project was simply too ambitious. The focus was narrowed to the creation of a development platform that would support the popular operating systems of the day, including OS/2, Windows, Mac, and Unix. But it was too late. In 1996, Taligent became a subsidiary of IBM. Two years later, the project was disbanded and the developers were integrated into IBM.[7]

Taligent is a good example of the silver bullet syndrome because it promised to easily transform the way software was developed—and then it couldn't deliver. But as with many technologies that over-promise, it offered important lessons about what it would take to develop a new generation of software with the flexibility that developers wanted and now take for granted. This approach is the foundation of innovations that are commonplace today. Everything from complex service-oriented architectures, to Web 2.0, to "mash-ups," Facebook, iTunes, and Google Applications—to name a few—owe a debt of gratitude to the hard work of silver bullet pioneers from earlier generations.

NAVIGATING A SILVER BULLET MARKET

It is very tricky to maneuver through an overhyped silver bullet market. Because there is so much excitement and abundant funding, it is tempting for emerging companies to invest time and money to become part of the market. Clearly there are good reasons for technology companies to position themselves as players in one of these exciting markets. After all, customers always want products that promise to improve their ability to beat their competitors. Clearly, too, many technology companies and their management teams have made huge profits by riding these waves. However, there are dangers as well. Because one of the main characteristics of a silver bullet market is an inevitable stage of disillusionment, companies have to recognize that trends come and go. These companies therefore need to position themselves broadly enough so that they are not captive to a single market. This isn't easy, but it is important. Clearly it is easier for very large companies to protect themselves against changes in markets. Companies like IBM, Microsoft, HP, and Cisco have a broad enough market position as technology leaders that they can invest in a silver bullet market without becoming captive to that market. For example, both IBM and Microsoft poured huge development and marketing resources into the client/server market and made huge amounts of money selling products to customers. When the market began to shift, they were able to take those assets and shift them into new product offerings so that they would be ready for the next wave. Smaller companies have a harder time adapting.

But a company does not have to be the size of an IBM or a Microsoft to survive a silver bullet market. For example, Intelli-Corp, which was founded in 1980 as an artificial intelligence company, managed to survive by applying its AI technology to a different market, the well-established enterprise resource planning (ERP) market.[8] Emerging companies have a difficult time surviving a silver bullet market because they rarely have an alternative approach to packaging their technology.

New technology innovations are transformative. There is energy and excitement in these markets—entrepreneurs and investors are energized, investors anticipate huge profits, customers see the answers to their problems. It is therefore easy to bet everything on one of these markets. It's even easier to bet everything and fail. But the traps of a silver bullet market are avoidable.

Lessons Learned

Lesson One: Keep perspective. When a new market begins to evolve, position your company and develop your technology so that you can compete without committing everything to a single market. For example, companies that positioned themselves as object-oriented tools companies failed when customers realized that a tool was only part of the solution. The companies that succeeded were companies like Apple and Google, which have successfully leveraged object-oriented technology across their product offerings to achieve significant growth.

Lesson Two: Remember the customer. Customers get excited about silver bullets because of the potential benefits to their companies, not because of the characteristics of the technology. So follow the pain, not the hype.

Lesson Three: It isn't all about you. When a company is lucky enough to gain success in a silver bullet market, it is easy to become immersed in this first wave of success. However, this early success may come at a big price. If you have to spend all of your time and money "educating the market," it is usually a sign that buyers are not ready. Newer companies with more mature technology will be able to leverage the work of early market innovators. Once the hype settles down and reality sets in, customers want a solution that doesn't create more problems than it solves. Customers want predictability, and they want their technology partner to make them successful.

Lesson Four: Make sure you're solving a real problem. One of the hardest problems for emerging companies is determining what is real and what is hype. Make sure you are solving a real business problem. Smart entrepreneurs figure out how to create a roadmap to continue to solve customer problems.

Silver bullets in the high-tech world are products and technologies that promise quick and easy solutions to customer problems but then fail to deliver on the promise. Vendors that fall into the trap of selling silver bullets are doomed to fail. But companies that use the lessons a silver bullet product or technology can teach us, and who build on those lessons, may achieve great success.

It's smarter to be lucky than it's lucky to be smart.
—King Charles in *Pippin*

Chapter Ten

SPLITTING UP IS HARD TO DO

When Walking Away from
Legacy Products Makes Sense

Companies that have legacy products often have a difficult time changing and innovating. The most difficult task for a technology company is to destroy an outdated product in order to bring about a potentially brighter future.

Technology products go through a predictable lifecycle. Products are often introduced with great fanfare and sold to early adopters. If these early experiments are successful, more customers buy, and soon, with some luck, the product becomes well established in the market. Before long, hundreds and perhaps thousands of companies rely on these products. Individuals build their knowledge base and their careers around managing these products for their companies. Whole ecosystems of partners, systems integrators, value-added resellers, repair companies, and consultants are connected to supporting that product.

A product doesn't become a legacy overnight. A legacy product is, by definition, outdated. Over time, new technology emerges that offers a better approach to solve customer problems and hence threatens a legacy. As this happens, customers begin to adopt the new approaches, and the old product is less important to the company's future opportunities. A legacy product is one that is no longer actively marketed but remains deeply entrenched with customers. Customers simply do not let go of the product they have grown dependent on to run their businesses. It isn't much of a mystery.

Say a company purchases a software product to solve a specific problem—managing accounting, handling customer support, or collaborating with key partners. The product is implemented and customized and becomes part of the fabric of corporate life. Managers know how to use the software, and IT knows how to support the product. But as technology changes, the software that was once new and competitive ages. The company that develops the software must be able to compete with emerging players that are creating new products with more advanced features. The company providing the legacy software has a significant problem: do they continue to support the products that are used by very few new customers, or do they choose to let those products die and move on to develop new ones? In the best of all possible worlds, the company might want to do both: support existing customers as long as necessary and invest in new competitive technology. However, it is difficult to fund the necessary support for both the old and the new.

There are three stages that take place when a start-up challenges the legacy product of a market incumbent:

> *Stage One.* The market incumbent's legacy product is challenged by a start-up with newer technology that solves one of the most complex problems that has plagued the market leader. Now prospective customers begin to rethink their acquisition strategy.

> *Stage Two.* The start-ups in the market are able to convince prospective customers to buy their offerings. Because these companies do not have the legacy of aging technology to contend with, the products are more attractive. The market

incumbent finds itself on the defensive and tries to either patch deficiencies in its offerings or sell aggressively against the challengers.

Stage Three. The sales pipeline of the incumbent vendor begins to shrink. Existing customers do not necessarily flee, as they may be dependent on the products to run some aspect of day-to-day operations, but they begin to move some critical aspects of those processes to newer technologies. Partners put pressure on the vendor to do something quickly to salvage their businesses. At the same time, these partners begin to look for alternative partner ecosystems so they can diversify with other product companies. At this point, a market incumbent has two choices: it can either continue to support existing customers, adding additional functionality and components, or it can begin to develop new product lines.

One of the most complicated transitions for technology vendors is to move away from products that over the years have been responsible for substantial revenue. But keeping old products alive with a dwindling customer base wastes energy and money that could be better spent investing in new products. The smartest companies are those that leverage their knowledge of customers, existing markets, and their own intellectual property to move forward. Sometimes this means being bold and walking away from existing products. When companies try to move to a completely different market, where they lack even basic knowledge, they often fail miserably. The trick is using the assets that are often buried in existing products to create competitive offerings. Knowing the difference between great products and great intellectual property can define success or failure.

When companies are hugely successful with a product over the long term, it is very difficult for them to change. But these companies tend to get themselves into trouble when they hang on too tightly to their position in the market. Leaders can mistake existing product implementation for strategy: "We deliver printed documents." "We sell databases." "We sell the lowest-priced personal computers." Although all of these statements might be true for various companies, they do not get at the core of the value that the companies bring to customers. In reality, leaders understand that they are selling the promise of streamlining how work is done in a way that allows their customers to be more successful by increasing revenue and improving efficiency. Therefore these vendors need to focus on the success of their customers. If the vendor instead bases its strategy solely on developing more sophisticated technology, the company will not grow.

Companies that stick to what they have done for years, without trying to match their core competency with customer problems, are destined to go out of business. These companies become trapped in their past and have trouble reinventing themselves. It is not easy to watch emerging companies take your market share when you are a recognized leader in a market. Yet this is precisely what happened to the companies described in Chapter One. Wang, Digital Equipment Corporation, and Sun simply were not able to leverage their strengths to adapt to the changing market, and emerging companies such as Google eventually made those companies irrelevant.

ENTERPRISE RESOURCE PLANNING:
THE VALUE OF MAINTENANCE REVENUE

Legacy products often have high profit margins because the cost of maintaining those products are relatively low. In addition, vendors (especially those with lots of customers) continue to collect maintenance fees every year. Such fees are almost pure profit. This is especially true for complex enterprise software products like the ERP products offered by SAP, Oracle, and others. The reality is that these products become so intertwined within the fabric of the business that it is very hard to dislodge them. This can certainly be a significant benefit to the vendor's bottom line. But many ERP companies have failed because they never moved beyond their original products. Once-prominent companies like Platinum and Baan Software were not able to change rapidly enough to survive. Others—such as PeopleSoft, JD Edwards, and Navision—were acquired. Vendors such as Oracle have done well by supporting these legacy enterprise applications—although rather than simply maintaining them in their current state, Oracle has bought a huge number of important enterprise applications and continued to improve and modernize them. Over time, Oracle intends to create a common set of components across the vast number of enterprise software technologies it has purchased in the past decade. But although inventive companies like Oracle have learned how to streamline products that are a drag on their future costs, Oracle tends to be the exception to the rule, and generally, legacy products do not easily evolve. Most companies have a difficult time supporting legacy products while at the same time transforming them to meet the needs of new customers looking for innovation.

Generally, vendors that have aging software tend to simply support their installed base of customers by fixing problems and incrementally adding new functions intended to keep the software running. Rather than focusing on change and innovation, they concentrate on this "easy money," thereby losing their competitive edge. Although the cash flow may keep a company in business, it won't produce enough revenue for future expansion—unless the company changes its strategy. In this situation, companies with aging legacy products usually need to eliminate old products in order to thrive in increasingly competitive markets. The most successful companies understand that their value to customers isn't necessarily in their existing products, but in the intellectual property embedded in those products.

AT&T: Forcing Change

One of my favorite examples of a company that transformed itself is AT&T. Back in the 1950s, AT&T was *the* telephone company.[1] It was, in essence, a utility protected against having to compete in the market. However, there was a crisis brewing. The phone network was aging and needed to be updated to meet the needs of emerging business requirements. How could company management motivate its employees to think boldly and reinvent itself—especially if there was no immediate competitive threat? This was no easy task. The way AT&T motivated its engineers to reinvent the phone system is a brilliant example of actively forcing change to happen.

During the '50s, in order to get its engineers to create a new and better telephone network, AT&T management called a meeting of its top engineering talent. As an experiment, the engineers were told that there had been a terrible explosion, damaging the phone network beyond repair. They were then tasked with designing a brand-new telephone network from scratch to replace the one that "no longer existed." Shielded from the outside world, they did indeed come up with a brand-new and innovative plan. Why the fictional crisis? The company needed to evolve the existing phone network in order to modernize it; they believed that the engineering team, given that task outright, would have simply used the existing network and tried to update it with new bells and whistles. It was clear to company management that success would require "destroying" the old system and thinking differently about the future—and their ploy seemed the most effective way to do that.

The subterfuge to which AT&T management felt it had to resort underscores the fact that change is difficult even when management wants change. And a technology company with an installed base of customers paying maintenance and upgrade fees will likely be reluctant to leave that comfort zone. This is understandable. Even if the company isn't growing, there is still money coming in. There are teams whose salaries and careers are built on supporting those products. There are loyal customers who insist that the company needs to continue to support them—no matter what happens.

Conventional wisdom would have you believe that the large companies are the ones that have the most trouble innovating and changing. The lumbering elephant moves slowly—that is the perception. In some ways, however, large companies are in the best position to change. After all, they have the resources to establish a small team of isolated developers to create new offerings. These offerings can be introduced without eliminating existing product lines. Similarly, very small market players are in a great position to kill existing offerings and respond to new opportunities because they don't have much to lose. It is the mid-sized companies—those without the financial resources of the giants or the freedom of the start-ups—that are most at risk. Such companies typically start during one of the overhyped markets, gain traction, and then tread water for decades.

Failure to change is almost always fatal. And given how complicated it can be for a company to change, there are more examples of failures than there are success stories. The industry is littered with disappointments, whether it is a mainframe software company that couldn't produce software solutions for new operating systems or hardware platforms or a telephone company that was trounced by more nimble competitors. Much less common is the company that was able to transform itself by destroying the products that made it successful and moving on to a brave new world.

There are several different approaches that large companies take to help themselves transform for the next generation of technology. Some companies simply discontinue an existing product and replace it with a new generation. Others purchase a successful company in a significant market niche and allow it to flourish on its own. This gives the larger company the revenue and time it needs to revamp its existing portfolio of products. It is also possible for companies to use their existing successful products as a launching pad to move in new directions, so that customers may not notice the dramatic change. Still others create a parallel product organization. Very large companies like IBM, Oracle, and SAP often acquire innovative emerging companies to help them remain competitive.

MICROSOFT: THE ADVANTAGE OF KILLING OFF THE CASH COW

When IBM introduced its personal computer in 1981, the company selected Microsoft as its operating supplier. Over the years, MS-DOS became the de facto standard operating system for the PC. For example, in 1992 almost 60 percent of all personal computers were shipped with Microsoft's MS-DOS operating system. Most hardware manufacturers shipped their PCs with MS-DOS preloaded. In addition, there were many thousands of applications designed specifically to work with MS-DOS. Through the 1990s, MS-DOS remained an extraordinarily important product, used by huge numbers of customers, partners, and software developers across the globe. Despite the popularity and this huge installed base, Microsoft transitioned from MS-DOS to Windows. Although Windows used some of the code from MS-DOS, Microsoft replaced MS-DOS in the market. There were customers, software developers, and channel partners that wanted Microsoft to continue to support MS-DOS.[2] However, the company stopped new development by 2000. In some ways, it was easy for Microsoft to kill MS-DOS. Microsoft had been working on two different ways to evolve MS-DOS—one was its partnership with IBM to design a brand new operating system called OS/2, the other was the Windows operating system designed as a replacement for DOS. Because OS/2 failed to achieve market momentum, Microsoft made

Windows its strategic platform for the future. By 2000, Windows had evolved to the point where a large number of software vendors had moved their existing and new product offerings to the Windows operating system. It was also able to exert pressure on its hardware partners to include Windows as the default operating system for its new products. Even at this point, there was still a huge installed base of customers that wanted to stay with MS-DOS. However, in order to move forward, Microsoft used its powerful position with hardware and software vendors to force its partners to move beyond the MS-DOS platform. Even if partners wanted to hold onto the MS-DOS operating system, they were not given that option by Microsoft.

HP: GETTING OUT OF THE INSTRUMENTATION MARKET

Today Hewlett Packard is the largest information technology company in the world, with a focus on computer hardware, storage systems, networks, printers, software, and services. However, when Hewlett Packard was founded in 1939, it concentrated on the electronic test equipment market. Over the next several decades HP evolved as it introduced new products for the emerging computer industry. By the 1990s it was becoming clear to HP's leadership that it had two different and distinct businesses: (1) the IT business and (2) the test and measurement business. Each of these businesses had distinct constituents and different technology requirements. HP could have decided to continue to run the test and measurement business as a separate subsidiary. However, in 1999 HP was in the midst of expanding its IT business through acquisitions such as Compaq Computer, Inc.—an IT major systems company. Therefore HP decided to spin off the test and measurement business into a separate company called Agilent Technologies. Agilent, which had more than $8 billion in revenue in 1998, went public in 1999.

At first glance it might appear that HP was letting go of a relatively large portion of revenue and intellectual property when it spun off what became Agilent.[3] HP's gross revenue in 1999 was $42.4 billion; thus Agilent represented a large percentage of HP's overall revenue. However, by disengaging from the test and measurement business, HP was able to put all of its energy into its core business. Likewise, Agilent, as a standalone company, was able to focus on manufacturing scientific instruments and a variety of products in the pharmaceutical and life sciences markets. HP realized that in order to survive and thrive it needed to focus on its strengths in the enterprise hardware and consumer computing business. Moving away from the test and measurement business enabled this transition to happen.

APPLE INC.: LEAVING THE HOBBY MARKET TO BECOME A MEDIA EMPIRE

One of the most dramatic examples in the industry of a company that walked away from a revenue driving legacy product is Apple. It is no accident that Apple changed its name from Apple Computer, Inc. to Apple Inc. in 2007. The company's early history was as a personal computer vendor. And in the 1980s the company was not alone. There were hundreds of companies that developed some innovative technology to first service the "hobbyists"—people whose jobs never required computer skills but who loved their computers anyway. Most of these early companies are gone. Computers from companies like Atari, Commodore, and Tandy are likely to be found only in a computer museum.

During Steve Jobs' absence from Apple the company's strategy began to unravel. When he returned in 1996 it wasn't clear what the strategic direction should be. One of the luckiest consequences of Jobs having left Apple was that he started a company called

NeXTSTEP.[4] Unlike Apple, NeXTSTEP was able to start from scratch to build a new generation platform. In developing this platform, Jobs' team had designed an elegant operating system that was modern and incredibly flexible. Many traditional operating systems were monolithic, so that making a change was a lengthy and complicated process. In contrast, NeXTSTEP combined the maturity of the Unix operating system with components from the most important new research in operating system technology. The operating system was innovative because it was designed with a very small central controlling unit that was intended to make it easy to add and subtract components for maximum flexibility. This made change very easy. The result was a modern, modular, and highly flexible operating system. It was therefore stable and scalable as well as easy to maintain. But because NeXTSTEP itself was ahead of its time, it did not have enough momentum to quickly become a major player. However, those individuals who had an opportunity to experiment with the platform saw the type of power the system could offer. Apple's management saw the potential of the struggling company and bought it. This acquisition brought Steve Jobs back to Apple, and when he returned, he realized that for the company to thrive it needed to differentiate itself for the future. Jobs therefore took the bold step of replacing the traditional operating system that was the foundation of all the company's products with the more advanced NeXTSTEP operating system.

The operating system is the nerve center of any technology. All technology innovations must have an operating system that tells the technology how to behave in many different situations. If it is well developed, it can be used in many different situations and can actually enhance a company's ability to transform the technology it brings to market. Companies that have rigid operating systems are often forced to build a new operating system—in essence, a new nervous system—each time they want to innovate. Not only does this affect time to market, but it also means that each of these products exists in isolation from the next product. With the advanced technology in the NeXT operating system, Apple now had the flexibility to be able to innovate in new ways. In a PC market that was dominated by commodity boxes and Microsoft's Windows operating system, the innovation of the NeXT operating system allowed Apple to move to a next-generation platform.

Apple was also able to use the same modular software development approach to develop the iPod, the iPhone, and the iPad. Because of the common underpinnings, these products address adjacent markets, so Apple can extend its relationship with existing customers in new ways. This has allowed the company to move its focus to devices that transcend the business and consumer markets. By killing off existing and lucrative products, Apple has been able to transform itself from a company that just sold computers to a technology company with offerings as diverse as tablet computers, smartphones, and a digital media store.

Although Apple may have made this kind of transformation look easy, it is far from simple to achieve. Even very large companies that have the ability to establish a separate development team to pursue new product strategies can fail. Too often, the politics of personality, power, and control can sabotage the best plans. What if a company leader is urged to move in two diametrically opposed directions by two different internal teams? Which one will win? Will it be the team with the most revolutionary plan? Will it be the team whose leader is best able to influence the CEO? There are countless examples of companies (as well as countries) that failed because the leaders listened to the wrong people, often with hidden agendas. So not only do companies have to contend with markets that are changing and innovations that seem to come out of nowhere, but they also have to make important judgment calls. Sometimes judgment and political forces trump innovation and reinvention.

SKUNKWORKS: ALLOWING NEW PRODUCTS
TO DEVELOP OUT OF THE SPOTLIGHT

One way that companies have tried to get around the politics of product development is through "skunkworks" projects. Skunkworks is an idea developed by Lockheed Martin. Indeed, Skunk Works is the registered mark for the company's Advanced Development Programs, which were designed to allow new development to be done outside of the traditional organizational structure. These projects have resulted in the development of many of Lockheed Martin's more innovative airplanes.[5] As you can imagine, the need to innovate and change complex airplane designs is extreme. How then, do you get people to try something completely different without a bureaucracy killing it off? The process at Lockheed was simple: select a team of smart people, take them out of their day-to-day tasks, and allow them to work independently to solve a discrete problem. They do not need to adhere to a production schedule or answer to other managers. If done well, skunkworks can have dramatically impressive results.

IBM has made significant changes in its business through skunkworks initiatives. When it became clear that there were key market drivers encouraging customers to abandon the mainframe computer, IBM took action to try to transform the platform to make it more relevant to existing and perhaps new customers. Like many legacy products, the mainframe was still responsible for billions of dollars of revenue and profit. IBM initiated a skunkworks project to implement the increasingly popular Linux operating system as a native operating system. Such a project could never have been handed over to the existing development team. It required different thinking and a different approach that was counterintuitive to that team. Most likely, the team that owed its livelihood to the existing mainframe operating system would have found a way to undermine the project and ensure its failure. By adding the Linux operating system as an option on the mainframe, IBM made this system more acceptable to customers who wanted the scalability of the mainframe but did not want to have to learn a proprietary operating system.

Lessons Learned

Lesson One: Think differently about success. Just because you have been an early innovator or a successful company in your market, it does not guarantee long-term longevity. Your most successful product could sow the seeds of your destruction. Sometimes killing off products helps a company enter new markets and focuses the company's energy and time on emerging customer needs.

Lesson Two: Know when to listen to customers. Most companies have customer councils and even huge departments that spend all of their time listening to customers. Although this can be useful, there are dangers. Loyal customers often don't want big change. They simply want you to make incremental changes to existing products. It may well be precisely the customers that have walked away from your products that you want to listen to. The people who won't buy from you today might be your best customers tomorrow. Listening to them might be an effective way to plan your strategy.

Lesson Three: Take start-ups seriously. The greatest threat to a dominant market player is a well-funded start-up with a blank slate. An installed base and great revenue do not guarantee success. A lucky start-up with a completely different model for solving customer problems can undermine even the strongest incumbent.

Lesson Four: Politics is toxic. Make business decisions based on objective analysis, not on which faction has the most power. It takes strong leadership to listen to those voices that disagree with long-held beliefs. It is dangerous when management listens only to people who already have the same views and beliefs. It is often more important to pay attention to those voices that are in conflict with conventional wisdom within your company. Someone with a different view may hold the strategy that can transform a company's fortunes. It is important to understand employees' motivations. Above all, concentrate on what customers need to achieve success in the future and on how your company can facilitate that success.

One of the most difficult things for successful companies to do is completely change direction. Resistance to change comes from customers who are comfortable with the status quo and from employees whose futures may be tied to existing products. Sometimes killing those products can unleash creativity and innovation. When that happens, a floundering company can turn into an industry leader, and a successful company can find even greater success.

CONCLUSION:
TEN RULES FOR TURNING LUCK
INTO SUSTAINABLE SUCCESS

Luck matters.

We like to think of our society as a meritocracy in which success comes to those who have superior abilities and are willing to work the hardest. But the fact of the matter is that luck often plays as great a role in success as do intelligence and hard work. This is particularly true in technology markets—luck plays an important but overlooked part in the success or failure of high-tech companies. And whether we are talking about start-ups or well-established companies, luck plays a key role in achieving and sustaining success.

Conventional wisdom tells us that smart entrepreneurs who come up with a sophisticated product and execute deftly should succeed. But history shows us that in technology markets, having a good product isn't enough. Many of the most innovative products don't even make it to the commercial market when they are initially invented. In fact, hundreds of great engineering and technology concepts take decades to develop before they achieve commercial success. Sometimes the stars need to be aligned in just the right way, so that customers with a problem to solve recognize the value of a new technology. Sometimes the underlying technology simply needs time to mature before customers will adopt it.

As we have seen, timing is everything. When I talk about luck in this context, I mean being in the right market at a time when potential customers are ready to use your product or service. But good luck is just the beginning of a successful enterprise. Other factors are necessary if a company is to sustain success. A company has to be smart enough to harness its luck to build a sustainable future.

To succeed with a new business, you need a plan for nurturing your ideas, your team, and your customers, so that you can sustain your growth over the long term. Your luck and smarts need to be in harmony. You need to be lucky enough that the market will need and understand your product. And you need to be smart enough to appreciate your luck so that you can turn that luck into long-term success.

For every company that is lucky enough and smart enough to achieve incredible riches, there are a hundred others that fail. The challenges differ, depending on your type of company, but they are always there. If you are a start-up with limited funding, you have to fight hard to gain traction. You have to convince prospective customers to take a chance with an unproven group of entrepreneurs and an unproven product. Also, if your technology brings a different approach to a customer problem, you have the challenge of getting customers to understand and appreciate the new approach. Customers don't buy what they don't understand. And even if you are skillful and lucky enough to convince customers to buy your products, you then have to anticipate how customers will actually use them. Often, customers will attempt to use your product to do something it was not designed for, and if that product isn't flexible enough to change as customer expectations change, you will not be able to sustain your early success. Emerging companies have the added difficulty of competing with market incumbents that have the customer relationships and the money to make life difficult for the upstart. To succeed, a start-up must be lucky enough to be ready just as market needs mature, nimble enough to respond to opportunities, creative enough to create new business models, humble enough to be willing to partner with others, and shrewd enough to withstand competitive pressures.

Contrast these challenges with those of an established technology company trying to gain momentum with new technology or a new market focus. While the start-up has a clean slate to innovate, the market incumbent has to fight against market perceptions and its own inertia. It often has an installed base of customers who are resistant to change and internal teams that don't see the need to change technology they are comfortable with. It therefore can be much harder for a market leader to move quickly when threatened with changing market dynamics. Mature companies often establish an independent team to develop a new product; such teams may escape the confines and complexity of working within an existing product area. Of course, established companies may also have sufficient cash to purchase a market leader in an emerging market and then allow that company to mature independently. The successful market incumbent uses a combination of the power of its brand, customer loyalty, and investment in the right technology to survive and thrive, and is also willing to empower internal entrepreneurs to lead the charge into the future.

To be successful, technology companies need to be smart enough to learn from both the successes and failures of the past. In fact, many successful companies today can trace their success to the effective leveraging of ideas, technologies, and approaches that had failed in an earlier time. Ironically, technology entrepreneurs are often unaware of lessons they can learn from earlier generations. However, as is demonstrated in the stories of the companies I have discussed in this book, moving from being lucky to being smart means learning the important lessons that history teaches us.

For almost thirty years I have observed and participated in the world of high tech. I have seen many successes, and even more failures. Patterns have emerged, and from these patterns I have gleaned some important rules for success.

Rule One: Follow the pain. Focus on the problems that your customers or prospects cannot solve right now. It doesn't matter whether you work for an established company or an emerging one—customers always need solutions that address their most important problems. This may sound like common sense, but too many technology companies become so focused on the intricacies of the code that they lose sight of the purpose of the technology. "If you can do that for me, I am interested . . . " are the only words that count when selling to prospects.

Rule Two: Know when and how to listen. Listening to the market, your customers, your prospects, and your own team can mean the difference between success and failure. I like the rule of three: if you hear the same issue discussed by three customers, three prospects, or three employees, there is an important issue emerging that will have consequences.

But listening *too* closely can also be risky. Make sure that you are not listening to the wrong voices. A few customers or prospects can give you a laundry list of functions that they would like to see your new product perform. Are these customer requirements widespread enough to help you sustain leadership? Listening to the wrong advice can cause you to focus on tactics rather than on new opportunities. Even if you are lucky enough to figure out precisely what customers really need to solve problems, you have to make your solutions approachable. As you focus on these opportunities, you have to make it easy for customers to adopt your technology quickly.

Emerging markets are always evolving. If a technology requirement has already become mainstream, it may be too late for you to have a major impact. But if you listen actively, you may be able to anticipate the future ahead of other market players.

Rule Three: Don't rest on your laurels. One of the biggest traps for a technology company is overconfidence. You are not guaranteed future success just because you are currently the market leader. It is never wise to assume that the past is a predictor of the future. The best companies are always looking ahead. Existing companies with strong revenue and a good installed base can either partner with or buy the best emerging companies to help create a secure future. A good technology market is never mature. It is always evolving. If the market you have been selling your products in is stagnant, it is time to change your approach.

Rule Four: Study your market carefully. Technology businesses tend to get consumed by internal issues like planning the launch of a product, opening sales offices, or working with potential partners. Although these day-to-day business issues are extremely important, entrepreneurs need to focus on the competitive market. You need to pay attention to what competitors are doing, what new players are entering the market, and what they are offering. Learn from the tactics and strategies of your competitors. You are most at risk when you first begin to gain market traction. When your company seems to come out of nowhere and suddenly gains the attention of prospects, financial analysts, and the press, your competitors will be watching. Plan your next moves by anticipating and understanding what your competitors might do as a reaction to your success.

Rule Five: Don't follow blindly. Emerging technology markets are exciting, and there is typically a lot of venture capital available. It is very easy for an entrepreneur to get caught up in the excitement without a well-thought-out plan for success. Don't simply rush into an emerging market with an un-differentiated product. To thrive, it is better to create a strategy that leverages an important technology but focuses on figuring out a solution to an unsolved need. Many entrepreneurs who discover a technique or winning approach are unprepared for competitive pressures. If lucky entrepreneurs with innovative products aren't prepared, they can be easily challenged by start-ups and aggressive market leaders. Successful entrepreneurs focus on creating sustainable companies rather than on hitting a quick jackpot.

Rule Six: Build relationships as diligently as you build technology. In an exciting, emerging market, you need all the friends you can get. There are a number of benefits that result from building relationships with important market influencers. First, you can get advice from both lucky and smart leaders who were once in the same position that you are in now. They have all learned important lessons that can spare you a lot of unnecessary pain. Second, leaders can introduce you to pro-spective customers; a recommendation—either explicit or implicit—can be critical in turning a prospect into a customer. Finally, relationships with important corporate leaders, press, analysts, bloggers, and social networkers are imperative in building a strong brand. The smartest technology companies are the ones that leverage their network of influencers to create momentum in the market.

Rule Seven: Focus on the value of technology to your customers, not on the pure value of your technology. Most technology companies plan to grow into a sustainable business by building on great technical expertise. So why do some companies get lucky with their products while others simply fade away? It has to do with the focus on customer needs. Technology is about applying best practices to solving an intractable problem and persuading a customer to pay for it. If you find that all of your discussions with your leadership team are about the technology, you may be losing sight of the big picture—what your customers need and how you can achieve revenue growth and business sustainability.

Rule Eight: Be prepared for perpetual change. The only certainty in expanding technology markets is that they will change. Therefore, even if your company has been lucky enough to emerge as an early leader, be prepared for new technology innovations, new competitors, and changing market conditions. The best strategy is to assume there will be change and to embrace changes enthusiastically. The companies that fail are the ones that fail to react to new conditions. Stay a step ahead, with a strategy based on continuously adapting.

Rule Nine: Embrace start-ups and their innovation. If you are lucky enough to have made it through the start-up phase and smart enough to become a player in an important emerging market, this is the time to look to new, emerging start-ups. Once you become an established company, you become much more consumed with the day-to-day requirements of managing growth, keeping customers happy, and overseeing the development process. Smart, established companies that hope to continue to survive and innovate will go out of their way to embrace emerging companies—as either partners or acquisitions.

Rule Ten: Apply knowledge to new markets in inventive ways. One of the most exciting opportunities in technology today is the chance to apply lessons learned in earlier markets to emerging ones. There may be an important technology used extensively in one market that can help transform a completely different market. Therefore, if you are building a new start-up, you can gain competitive advantage by applying a great technology in a completely different way.

It's time to get smart! There are wonderful opportunities to leverage the lessons learned in technology industries over the last several decades. Entrepreneurs have never been in a better position to channel their luck to solve real customer problems in new ways. Leverage the knowledge in the market, anticipate change, listen, learn, experiment, and change the world.

NOTES

CHAPTER ONE

1. Computer Museum, *The History of Computing: An Encyclopedia of the People and Machines That Made Computer History.* Lexikon Services, 1982–2003, http://www.computermuseum.li/Testpage/Wang Getronics.htm.
2. An Wang, *Lessons: An Autobiography* (Reading, MA: Addison Wesley, 1986).
3. Charles Kenney, *Riding the Runaway Horse: The Rise and Decline of Wang Laboratories* (Boston: Little, Brown, 1992).
4. James Redin, "The Doctor and His Calculator," http://www.xnumber.com/xnumber/anwang.htm.
5. "Slipping Beyond the Bottom Line." *Time*, August 31, 1992.
6. Edgar Schein, *DEC Is Dead, Long Live DEC: The Lasting Legacy of Digital Equipment Corp* (San Francisco: Berrett-Koehler, 2003).
7. Jeffrey R. Yost, *The Computer Industry* (Westport, CT: Greenwood Press, 2005).
8. Paul E. Ceruzzi, *A History of Modern Computing* (Cambridge, MA: MIT Press, 2003).
9. Tom Kranz, "History of Sun Microsystems." EzineArticles.com, November 7, 2008, http://ezinearticles.com/?The-History-of-Sun-Microsystems&id=1665583.
10. Apollo Computer, http://en.wikipedia.org/wiki/Apollo_Computer.
11. Ibid.
12. Brent Schlender, "JavaMan, The Adventures of Scott McNealy." *Fortune,* October 13, 1997.

13. Adam Hartung, "Why Sun Failed to Adapt." The Phoenix Principle blog, April 21, 2009.
14. Dana Gardner, "Sun's Forte Purchase Fills Out Java Tools Line." *InfoWorld*, August 30, 1999, p. 12.
15. C. Gordon Bell, *High-Tech Ventures: The Guide for Entrepreneurial Success* (New York: Basic Books, 1991).

Chapter Two

1. Martin Marshall, "The Battle over Motif Management." *InfoWorld*, May 14, 1990.
2. Martin Marshall, "Visix Previews Looking Glass at Show." *InfoWorld*, June 4, 1990.
3. Cate Corcoran, "Visix to Ship High Octane Development Tools." *InfoWorld*, September 21, 1992.
4. Keven Bodner, "Vibe Creates Sophisticated Apps." *InfoWorld*, April 14, 1997.
5. Stewart Deck, "Visix to Shut Its Doors." *Computerworld*, March 25, 1998.
6. *Visual Basic/History*. Wikibooks Wikimedia Foundation.
7. Judith Hurwitz, Marcia Kaufman, Fern Halper, and Robin Bloor, *Cloud Computing for Dummies* (Hoboken, NJ: Wiley, 2009).

Chapter Three

1. IBM Archives, http://www-03.ibm.com/ibm/history/documents/index.html.
2. John Burgess, "IBM's $5 Billion Loss Highest in American Corporate History." *Washington Post*, January 20, 1993.
3. D. Quinn Mills and G. Bruce Friesen, *Broken Promises: An Unconventional View of What Went Wrong at IBM* (Cambridge, MA: Harvard Business School Press, 1996).

4. Ibid.

5. Ibid.

6. Robert X. Cringely, "Fixing IBM: Big Blue Has Big Problems." The Pulpit weekly column, Public Broadcasting Service, April 18, 2002, http://www.pbs.org/cringely/pulpit/2002/pulpit_20020418_000729 .html.

7. Louis V. Gerstner, Jr., *Who Says Elephants Can't Dance? Inside IBM's Historic Turnaround* (New York: Collins, 2002).

8. Katie Hoffman, "IBM Shareholders See Stability in Palmisano Staying on as CEO." Bloomberg News, September 15, 2010, http://www .bloomberg.com/news/2010–09–14/ibm-s-sam-palmisano-says-policy- of-retirement-at-60-isn-t-cast-in-stone-.html.

9. Christopher Dernbach, "The History of the Apple Macintosh – Facts, Tales, and Stories About Apple and the Mac." Mac history website, collected and written by Christoph Dernbach, http://www.mac- history.net/.

10. Ibid.

11. Kimmy Powell, "Tech Tip 90 – An Insanely Great Thirty Years of Innovation. A Brief History of Apple Computers." Geeks.com, August 2006, http://www.geeks.com/techtips/2006/techtips-10aug 06.htm.

12. Tom Hormby, "The Story Behind Apple's 1984 Ad." Tom Hormby's Orchard blog, http://lowendmac.com/orchard/06/1984-apple-superbowl- ad.html.

13. TUAW (The Unoffical Apple Weblog), http://www.tuaw.com/2010/ 10/14/john-sculley-on-steve-jobs-guiding-principles/.

14. Daniel Eran Dilger, "The Apple Market Share Myth." Roughly Drafted blog, July 21, 2006, http://www.roughlydrafted.com/RD/ Home/D579148C-8563–4FFB-8E97-C2613215F98E.html.

15. Powell, "Tech Tip 90."

16. Cringely, "Fixing IBM."

17. TUAW.

18. Powell, "Tech Tip 90."

19. Ibid.

Chapter Four

1. "Mosaic Communications Changes Name to 'Netscape Communications Corporation.'" Press release, 1995, http://www.holgermetzger.de/netscape/NetscapeCommunicationsNewsRelease.htm.
2. James Collins, Marc Hequet, David Jackson, Stacy Perman, and Adam Zagorin, "Netscape's Marc Andreessen." *Time*, February 19, 1996.
3. David Becker, "Is This the End of Netscape?" *CNET News*, May 29, 2003.
4. "Mosaic Communications Changes Name."
5. Adam Lashinsky, "Remembering Netscape: The Birth of the Web." *Fortune*, July 25, 2005.
6. Ryan Naraine, "Netscape Death Is Long Overdue, Good for Security." *eWeek*, December 28, 2007.
7. Sandeep Junnarkar and Tim Clark, "AOL Buys Netscape for $4.2 Billion." *CNET News*, November 24, 1998.
8. Ibid.
9. John Battelle, "The Birth of Google." *Wired*, August 2005.
10. "Our Philosophy," http://www.google.com/corporate/tenthings.html.
11. Lawrence Page, Sergey Brin, Rajeev Motwani, and Terry Winograd, *The PageRank Citation Ranking: Bringing Order to the Web*. Technical report, Stanford InfoLab, 1999.
12. Randall Stross, *Planet Google: One Company's Audacious Plan to Organize Everything We Know* (New York: Free Press, 2008).
13. Lev Grossman and Andrea Sachs, "Is Amazon Taking Over the Book Business?" *Time*, June 22, 2009.
14. Page and others, *The PageRank Citation Ranking*.
15. Ibid.
16. Ibid.
17. Biography of Jeff Bezos, http://www.achievement.org/autodoc/page/bez0bio-1.
18. Fred Vogelstein, "Mighty Amazon." *Fortune*, May 26, 2003.
19. Biography of Jeff Bezos.
20. Ibid.

Chapter Five

1. "Sybase to Gobble Up Powersoft: What's Behind the Billion-Dollar Deal?" *Computer Industry Report*, November 18, 1994.
2. Patrick Lannigan, PowerBuilder History. Powersoft History blog, Fall 2004, http://www.lannigan.org/powersoft_powerbuilder_history.htm.
3. Mike Bucken, "Powersoft Gearing Up Development to Defend Early Lead—Powersoft Corp.'s Client/Server Development Software." *Software*, May 15, 1993.
4. Jacques Surveyer, "PowerBuilder Power++ 2.0." *Dr. Dobb's Journal*, December 1, 1997, http://www.drdobbs.com/184415592.
5. Ibid.
6. Rich Bianco, "The PowerBuilder Phenomenon – One Perspective." The Displaced Guy blog, March 25, 2010.
7. Gupta Technologies description, http://en.academic.ru/dic.nsf/enwiki/4966976.
8. "Interview with Umang Gupta." *DBMS*, February 1990.
9. Jeff Luther's Unify/Gupta/Centura Team Developer, Information and Sample Code Page, http://www.jeffluther.net/unify/#top.
10. Surveyer, "PowerBuilder Power++ 2.0."
11. Gupta Technologies overview, Wikipedia, http://en.wikipedia.org/wiki/Gupta_Technologies.

Chapter Six

1. "Frank Moss . . . " *Network World* briefs, November 2, 1998, p. 35.
2. Denise Pappalardo, "New ASP Agillion Ready to Talk About Services." *Network World*, September 13, 1999, p. 144.
3. Ibid.
4. Greg Alwang, "Agillion." *PC Magazine*, September 19, 2000.
5. "Agillion Recognized as an Upside Hot 100 Company; Austin Start-Up Recognized as Business-to-Business Leader." Press release, May 2000.

6. Jennifer Mears, "Faltering ASPs Rethink Business Plan." *Network World*, April 9, 2001, p. 12.

7. Broadband Sports SEC S-1 filing, November 26, 1999 (EDGAR Online).

8. "ESPN.com and Broadband Sports Team Up for Athletes Channel." Press release, November 20, 2000.

9. Stefanie Olsen, "Online Sports Network Shutters Sites." *CNET News*, February 16, 2001.

10. Kenneth Gilpin, "From a Giant Job to an Internet Fledgling." *New York Times*, October 27, 1999.

11. Excite background from Wikipedia.org.

12. @Home Networks background from Wikipedia.org.

13. Michael Noer, "Excite@Home Was Always a Bad Idea." Forbes.com, November 1, 2001.

14. Rachel Konrad, Corey Grice, and John Borland, "Was Excite@Home Marriage Doomed at the Altar?" *CNET News*, August 31, 2001.

Chapter Seven

1. Timeline: A Brief History of Artificial Intelligence, http://www.aaai.org/AITopics/pmwiki/pmwiki.php/AITopics/BriefHistory.

2. Lisa DiCarlo, "The Rebirth of Artificial Intelligence." Forbes.com, May 16, 2000.

3. Marty Sprinzen, "Components: Building Blocks for Automated Business Processes, Technology of Object-Oriented Languages." TOOLS 26 Proceedings, August 3–7, 1998.

4. The Open Group, timeline of Unix, http://www.unix.org/what_is_unix/history_timeline.html.

5. "Forte Software Announces Additional Equity Financing; Company Raises $10 Million to Expand." Business Wire press release, November 9, 1994.

6. Patrick L. Porter, "The Falcon Has Landed—Forte Software Pres. Marty Sprinzen." Editorial and brief article, *Software*, December 1996.

7. Mike Ricciuti and Stephen Shankland, "Sun's Forte Buy Gives Server Software a Boost." *CNET News,* August 23, 1999.
8. Michael Lyons bio, http://www.validshield.com/management.html.
9. Ibid.
10. Bob Brown, "Start-up Eyes Client/Server Dynasty." *Network World,* September 13, 1993.

CHAPTER EIGHT

1. "May Day! Hallmark's Site Down on V-Day." *Fast Company* staff blog, February 2005, http://www.fastcompany.com/blog/fast-company-staff/fast-company-blog/may-day-hallmarks-site-down-v-day.
2. John McCarthy, "Reminiscences on the History of Time Sharing." John McCarthy, Stanford University, Winter 1983, http://www-formal.stanford.edu/jmc/history/timesharing/timesharing.html.
3. Siebel history from Wikipedia.org.
4. Jonathan Skillings, "Long Road for Siebel Ends at Oracle." ZDNet blog, September 12, 2005.
5. Marc Benioff bio, www.salesforce.com.
6. Marc Benioff and Carlyne Adler, *Behind the Cloud: The Untold Story of How Salesforce.com Went from Idea to Billion-Dollar Company and Revolutionized an Industry* (San Francisco: Jossey-Bass, 2009).
7. www.zoho.com.

CHAPTER NINE

1. Fred Brooks, *The Mythical Man-Month: Essays on Software Engineering,* 2nd ed. (Reading, MA: Addison-Wesley Professional, 1995).
2. "A Brief History of Object Oriented Programming" (n.d.), http://web.eecs.utk.edu/~huangj/CS302S04/notes/oo-intro.html.
3. "The Object of Venture Capital." Red Herring.com, October 31, 1993.
4. Paul Saffo, "Establish Giants Seeking Relief Create Industry Implosion." *InfoWorld,* July 22, 1991, p. 50.

5. John Hagedoorn, Elias Carayannis, and Jeffrey Alexander. "Strange Bedfellows in the Personal Computer Industry: Technology Alliances Between IBM and Apple." Report, February 2000, http://ideas.repec .org/p/dgr/umamer/2000011.html.
6. John Markoff, "Apple and IBM Offer Look at Their Microsoft Challenge." *New York Times,* March 22, 1994.
7. "IBM Is Set to Acquire New Subsidiary." Reuters, December 20, 1995.
8. Alice Leplant, "Bring in the Expert: Expert Systems Can't Solve All the Problems, But They Are Learning." *InfoWorld,* October 1, 1990, p. 55.

CHAPTER TEN

1. "History of the AT&T Network" (n.d.), http://www.corp.att.com/ history/nethistory/.
2. D. Rosenbaum, *Market Dominance: How Firms Gain, Hold, or Lose It and the Impact on Economic Performance* (Westport, CT: Praeger, 1998).
3. Stephen Shankland, "HP Names Spinoff Agilent." *CNET News,* July 28, 1999.
4. Tom Hormby, "NeXT, OpenStep, and the Triumphant Return of Steve Jobs." Tom Hormby's Orchard blog, November 15, 2005, http://lowendmac.com/orchard/05/next-acquisition.html.
5. "SKUNK WORKS: The Origin Story," http://www.lockheedmartin .com/aeronautics/skunkworks/.

ACKNOWLEDGMENTS

The adventure of writing *Smart or Lucky?* has been a long trek, sometimes over difficult terrain, but fortunately, I did not undertake this journey alone. Over many years, I was lucky to have the friendship, guidance, and insights of many teachers, professional colleagues, and family members. And I was smart enough to pay attention to them and learn from them.

First, I want to thank my husband, Warren. He has always been the person in my life who has given me the courage to take risks and to go in new directions. Without him, this book would never have been written. He was my primary editor, dedicating weekends and evenings to discussing ideas, reviewing text, and revising the manuscript. He never allowed me to settle for making this book anything less than the best it could be. Warren is my best friend and mentor. He has always urged me to take new directions with my career and has helped me to accomplish things I never thought I would be able to do.

I also want to thank my late father, David, who died much too young. He was a compassionate psychologist who was able to translate his techniques and philosophies into three books. I somehow knew that he expected me to do the same. He was a great teacher and a great visionary, and I miss him greatly. My mother, Elaine, also inspired me. She went to graduate school in her 40s, earning both a master's degree and a doctorate, and taught several generations of students at Massachusetts Bay Community College. She and my father wrote a book together on marriage and the family. Her love of learning, her tenacity, and her positive attitude have inspired me. My two children, Sara and David, are the lights of my life. They have grown into two beautiful and extraordinary individuals of whom I am very proud.

Marcia Kaufman, my business partner at Hurwitz & Associates for the past eight years, has been a tremendous help in sharing ideas that have made this book better. Her insights, energy, analytic mind, friendship, and support have been extraordinary. Fern Halper, my other business partner and colleague for more than fifteen years, provided ideas and analytical insights as well as friendship for which I will always be grateful.

There are thousands of entrepreneurs and technology leaders that I have met, consulted with, encouraged, and even disagreed with throughout my career. Each of these leaders has helped me refine my own thinking in a field that captivated me before I ever realized the potential of technology to change the world dramatically. I have observed the rise of many successful companies, and the failure of even more ventures. Every case has taught me important lessons, which became the raw material for this book.

Finally, I want to thank the people at Wiley, especially my editor, Karen Murphy, who accepted this book and guided me through the process. I also wish to express my gratitude to Katie Feltman, my editor for the four *For Dummies* books that my team at Hurwitz & Associates wrote, for her encouragement and assistance.

Judith Hurwitz
January 2011

ABOUT THE AUTHOR

Judith Hurwitz is president and CEO of Hurwitz & Associates, Inc., a strategy consulting and research firm focused on the business value of emerging computing technologies. She is a published author and a renowned industry pundit, providing strategic direction for and industry insight into many of the major technology players. Hurwitz is known as a no-holds-barred consultant who tells it like it is—whether that means telling an executive of a Fortune 500 software company that their strategy is lame or predicting the success or failure of a company coming out of left field. Because of her candor, she has been highly sought after for her insights and ability to provide strategic guidance. In 1996 *BusinessWeek* magazine named her as one of the top one hundred women in the computer industry; in 1997 she was named one of the top one hundred intriguing women by *Boston Magazine*. Hurwitz was named a distinguished alumnus of Boston University's College of Arts & Sciences in 2005 and is also a recipient of the 2005 Massachusetts Technology Leadership Council award. Hurwitz holds B.S. and M.S. degrees from Boston University, serves on several advisory boards of emerging companies, and has started three consulting firms over the past eighteen years. Along with her team at Hurwitz & Associates, she has authored several books in the *For Dummies* series, including *Cloud Computing for*

Dummies, Service Oriented Architecture for Dummies, and *Service Management for Dummies.* She also writes a popular technology blog—Judith Hurwitz's Cloud-Centric Weblog—and has published hundreds of articles and reports covering the computer industry.

INDEX